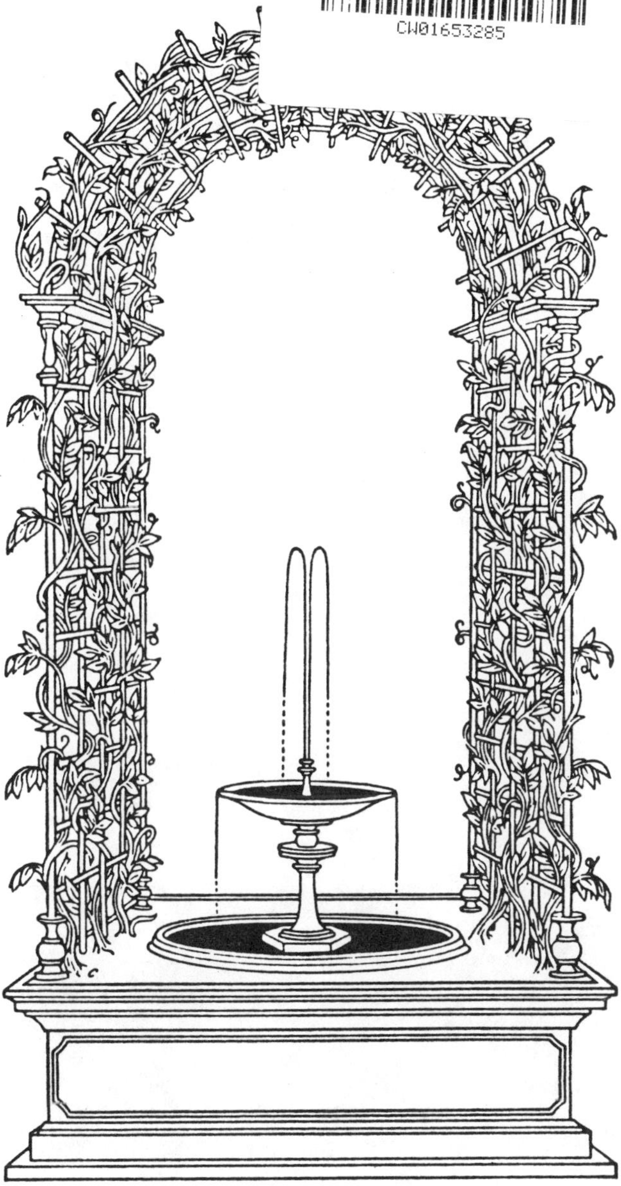

# *Serene Reflection Meditation*

# Serene Reflection Meditation

by

Rev. Master

P.T.N.H. Jiyu-Kennett, M.O.B.C.

and

Monks of the
Order of Buddhist Contemplatives

Shasta Abbey, Mt. Shasta, California.

*Frontispiece:* detail of a portrait of Shakyamuni Buddha;
painted by the 17th century artist
Cheng Chung, Ming dynasty (1368-1644).
From the collection of the National Palace Museum,
Taipei, Taiwan, Republic of China.

*Poem* (opposite page one):
by Rev. Master Jiyu-Kennett, M.O.B.C.,
and Rev. Kinzan Learman, M.O.B.C.;
based upon the first four sections of chapter VIII
of the *Udāna Scripture*.

ISBN 0-930066-11-1

Fifth edition revised—November 1989
First printing—November 1989

Originally published in 1974
as *Zen Meditation,* with revised second and third
editions in 1976 and 1980. The fourth revised edition was
published in England in 1987 as *Serene Reflection Meditation.* 
Printed in the United States of America.

*To my ordination master,*
*Rev. Seck Kim Seng.*

# *Contents.*

*Rules for Meditation.*
*Great Master Dōgen* 1

Commentary on Dōgen's *Rules for Meditation.*
*Rev. Master Jiyu-Kennett, M.O.B.C., Abbess* 4

How to Sit.
*Rev. Master Jiyu-Kennett, M.O.B.C., Abbess* 9

Concerning the Correct Use of the Sword of Buddha's Wisdom.
*Rev. Master Jiyu-Kennett, M.O.B.C., Abbess* 16

Serene Reflection.
*Rev. Kōten Benson, M.O.B.C.* 19

Physical Postures for Meditation.
*Rev. Daishin Morgan, M.O.B.C.* 22

The Mind of Meditation.
*Rev. Daishin Morgan, M.O.B.C.* 31

Obstacles in Meditation Practice.
*Rev. Kōshin Schomberg, M.O.B.C.* 38

Possible Physical Problems Met with in Meditation.
*Peter Lavin, Lay Minister, O.B.C.* 43

Your Place of Meditation.
*Rev. Shikō Rom, F.O.B.C.* 46

Children and Meditation.
*Rev. Master Jiyu-Kennett, M.O.B.C., Abbess* 52

Every-minute Meditation.
*Rev. Daizui MacPhillamy, M.O.B.C.* 54

Applying Meditation to Everyday Life.
*Rev. Jishō Perry, M.O.B.C.* 59

*The Kyojūkaimon and Commentary.*
*Great Master Keizan and Rev. Master Jiyu-Kennett, M.O.B.C., Abbess* 66

Reading *The Kyojūkaimon and Commentary.*
*David Powers, Lay Minister, O.B.C.* 77

The Practice of Wisdom.
*Rev. Kinzan Learman, M.O.B.C.* 81

The Ten Precepts Retreat: the Ceremony of Daily Life.
*Rev. Ekō Little, M.O.B.C.* 88

About Shasta Abbey. 101

*There is, O monks, an Unborn,*
*Uncreated, Unchanging, Undying.*
*If this were not so, O monks,*
*no end to birth, disease, old age, death.*

*Difficult It is to find;*
*the Unborn is no easy thing to know.*
*Craving's pierced by him who sees;*
*for him, no self or selfishness: repose.*

# *Rules for Meditation.*

*[This scripture was written by Great Master Dōgen, the founder of the Serene Reflection Meditation tradition in Japan. It is studied in great detail and recited daily at mid-day service in churches and monasteries of the Serene Reflection Meditation tradition.]*[1]

Why are training and enlightenment differentiated since the Truth is universal? Why study the means of attaining it since the supreme teaching is free? Since Truth is seen to be clearly apart from that which is unclean, why cling to a means of cleansing it? Since Truth is not separate from training, training is unnecessary—however, the separation would be as that between heaven and earth if even the slightest gap exists FOR, WHEN THE OPPOSITES ARISE, THE BUDDHA MIND IS LOST. However much you may be proud of your understanding, however much you may be enlightened, whatever your attainment of wisdom and supernatural power, your finding of the way to mind illumination, your power to touch heaven and to enter into enlightenment, when the opposites arise you have almost lost the way to salvation. Although the Buddha had great wisdom at birth, He sat in training for six years; although Bodhidharma Transmitted the Buddha Mind, we still hear the echoes of his nine years facing a wall. The Ancestors were very diligent and there is no reason why we people of the present day cannot understand. All you have to do is cease from erudition, withdraw within and reflect upon yourself. Should you be able to cast off body and mind naturally, the Buddha Mind will immediately manifest itself; if you want to find it quickly, you must start at once.

You should meditate in a quiet room, eat and drink moderately, cut all ties, give up everything, think of neither good nor evil, consider neither right nor wrong. Control mind function, will, consciousness, memory, perception and understanding; you must not strive thus to become Buddha. Cling to neither sitting nor lying down. When meditating do not wear tight clothing. Rest the left hand in the palm of the right hand with the thumbs touching lightly; sit upright, leaning neither to left nor right, backwards nor forwards. The ears must be in line with the shoulders and the nose in line with the navel; the tongue must be held lightly against the back of the top teeth with the lips and teeth closed. Keep the eyes open, breathe in quickly, settle the body comfortably and breathe out sharply. Sway the body left and right then sit steadily, neither trying to think nor trying not to think; just sitting, with no deliberate thought, is the important aspect of serene reflection meditation.

This type of meditation is not something that is done in stages; it is simply the lawful gateway to carefree peace. To train and enlighten ourselves is to become thoroughly wise; the kōan appears *naturally* in daily life. If you become thus utterly free you will be as the water wherein the dragon dwells or as the mountain whereon the tiger roams. Understand clearly that the Truth appears naturally and then your mind will be free from doubts and vacillation. When you wish to arise from meditation, sway the body gently from side to side and arise quietly; the body must make no violent movement; I myself have seen that the ability to die whilst sitting and standing, which transcends both peasant and sage, is obtained through the power of serene reflection meditation. It is no more possible to understand natural activity with the judgemental mind than it is possible to understand the signs of enlightenment; nor is it possible to understand training and enlightenment by supernatural means; such understanding is outside the realm of speech and vision, such Truth is beyond personal opinions. Do not discuss the wise and the ignorant, there is only one thing—to train hard for this is true enlightenment; training and enlightenment are naturally undefiled; to live in this way is the same as to live an ordinary daily life. The Buddha Seal has been preserved by both the Buddhas in the present world and by those in the world of the Indian and Chinese Ancestors, they are thus always spreading the Truth—*all* activity is permeated with pure meditation—the means of training are thousandfold but pure meditation must be done. It is futile to travel to other dusty countries thus forsaking your own seat; if your first step is false, you will immediately stumble. Already you are in possession of

*Serene reflection meditation.*

the vital attributes of a human being—do not waste time with this and that—*you* can possess the authority of Buddha. Of what use is it to merely enjoy this fleeting world? This body is as transient as dew on the grass, life passes as swiftly as a flash of lightning, quickly the body passes away, in a moment life is gone. O sincere trainees, do not doubt the true dragon, do not spend so much time in rubbing only a part of the elephant; look *inwards* and advance directly along the road that leads to the Mind, respect those who have reached the goal of goallessness, become one with the wisdom of the Buddhas, *Transmit* the wisdom of the Ancestors. If you do these things for some time you will become as herein described and then the Treasure House will open naturally and you will enjoy it fully.

* * *

*Note.*

1. We have removed the sections that describe meditation in cross-legged positions from the *Rules for Meditation*. Rev. Master Jiyu-Kennett explains: "We found that this type of sitting, when practiced by people who sat alone, injured too many legs and backs. If there are persons who would really like to learn this method we can show it to them but we are keeping it out of the *Rules for Meditation* from here on so that people do not suffer from the idea that this is the only way to go; there are other methods and they are just as effective and a lot safer for western people."

# *Commentary on Dōgen's Rules for Meditation.*

Rev. Master Jiyu-Kennett, M.O.B.C., Abbess

If you wish to harmonise body and mind it is absolutely imperative that you study the *Rules for Meditation* in detail. First, and foremost, keep your eyes open—otherwise you can get into a trance state in which you can accidentally die.

Second, control mind function, will, consciousness, memory, perception and understanding—if any one of these is allowed to predominate the balance and rhythm of the meditation will be upset and you will get nowhere. Be alert enough so that, whenever one or the other of these conditions begins to appear, you do not become attached to it so that you follow it to the detriment of the meditation; awareness is the key-word here.

Third, it does not matter whether you are sitting or lying down although the latter should only be used constantly if you are sick; laziness must be guarded against at all times; right effort is always required.

Fourth, do not worry about thoughts coming and going; just do not grab at them and do not push them away; watch them flow by naturally and do not be concerned with or interested in them.

Reprinted from Rev. Rōshi Jiyu-Kennett's *How to Grow a Lotus Blossom or How a Zen Buddhist Prepares for Death* (Mt. Shasta, California: Shasta Abbey Press, 1977), pp. 186-190.

Fifth, take two or three deep breaths when you start to meditate and then allow the breathing to become natural; do not try to make it different from what is natural breathing for you. Correct breathing is absolutely essential if one would meditate properly and this is only achieved if the meditator knows how to follow the breath properly. If one would follow the breath properly one must, as it states at the beginning of the *Rules for Meditation,* take two or three good breaths and then remain sitting quietly, allowing the breath to be perfectly natural. But not nearly enough has been said about these two or three 'good breaths' because it is not the depth of the breath but the path it takes that is absolutely essential to proper meditation.

Because of the mistakes made with regard to the last mentioned this commentary is chiefly concerned with how to take those two or three deep breaths.

Shakyamuni Buddha, after trying many harsh disciplines, and finding them useless, decided to try the method of breathing He had used as a child of seven. He was immediately successful in His attempts to reach enlightenment; He succeeded that very same night. Every small child knows how to meditate properly; it is only after we have "educated" it that its body and mind become separated and this was just as true of Shakyamuni Buddha as it is of us. This separation of body and mind can be precipitated by many things besides "education"; anything, in fact, that instils greed for worldly gain through competitiveness (the main cause of the disharmony of body and mind and its resulting tensions which ultimately lead to ill-health). Constantly quarrelling parents, or parents that do not make a secure home for their children, can cause the separation a lot earlier than the age of seven. This being so, he who would meditate properly must set up the breathing pattern that he used as a child. Here is how it is done.

The breath originates in the hara, an area roughly triangular in shape with its base in the area of the navel and its apex at the base of the sternum, the sides roughly corresponding to the sides of the rib cage. One should not count breaths when meditating; one should *follow the course* that the breath takes. Most people breathe without thinking about it but the meditator must *consciously*, at the *beginning* of each meditation, as well as at any time he *loses* his awareness during that meditation, *follow one or two* breaths thus:– Imagine, when taking these breaths, that at inhalation the breath starts at the base of the spine, continues up the spine and does not cease to move until it reaches the crown of the head which is the moment at which exhalation begins. The breath then continues down the front of the body during exhalation to the pubic area where inhalation takes over at the base of the spine. Thus the breath seems to travel in a circle, inhalation up the back of the body and exhalation down the front; it is *absolutely vital* that it travels up the spine and down the sternum.

This circular breathing is called "the turning of the Wheel of the Law"— and there is good reason for the name! If you set this back-flowing wheel, as it were, in motion during these two or three breaths then the whole pattern for meditation is correctly set and the breath will flow clearly, cleanly, and correctly and the meditation will be full and adequate.

There are some other things of importance here: in *meditation* this following of the breath is done consciously *two or three times* so that the breathing pattern may be established both physically and psychologically and then it must be *left behind* and the breathing allowed to settle *naturally* into the rhythm that is right for the individual. Above all, *do not* try to follow the breath in this way during the entire meditation. That pattern should only be set up again if the mind wanders much or if the mind falls out of meditation; then two or three more breaths should be taken in the same way and the pattern again set up.

When one finds that this type of breathing is so natural that it is second-nature to him he will notice that there are tiny fractions of time, called the 'apertures' in the breath, between inhalation and exhalation. If he has been able to learn how not to be distracted by his thoughts he will be still enough to hear the still, small voice, the voice of the Lord of the House,[1] during these tiny intervals: it is by means of listening to the Lord in these small intervals that body and mind once again enter into harmony.

When a person has become good at meditating in this way, which is nothing other than sitting quietly as the *Rules for Meditation* state, he will find that he can hear the still, small voice in other places. When he is good at this the still, small voice, his true nature, will take over from the voice of his egocentric ego—the roles that these two have played since the meditator suffered the disharmony of body and mind as a child will be reversed and then genuine spiritual progress is possible. The Christians call this state 'having conversations with God'; the Buddhist calls it the harmonisation of body and mind—it is explained elaborately in the Goi theory of Tōzan.[2] The *Sandōkai*[3] should be studied deeply in connection with this.

Understand that none of the above can take place until the involvement in the noise of the human brain dies down; a person who is constantly chasing after his own thoughts and getting involved with them will be too busy to hear the Lord of the House!

* * *

*Notes.*

1. See Great Master Keizan's "Denkōroku" ("The Transmission of the Light"), chapters 1, 2 and 7 in *Zen is Eternal Life* by Rōshi P.T.N.H. Jiyu-Kennett, 3rd ed. rev. (Mt. Shasta, California: Shasta Abbey Press, 1987).
2. The teaching of the Five Ranks by Great Master Tōzan Ryokai, the founder of the Serene Reflection Meditation tradition in China, describes the relationship of the Eternal and the Apparent.
3. A Scripture by Great Master Sekitō Kisen that describes the harmonisation of the "all is one" with the "all is different"; a translation of it is to be found in Rev. Master P.T.N.H. Jiyu-Kennett, M.O.B.C., *The Liturgy of the Order of Buddhist Contemplatives for the Laity* (Mt. Shasta, California: Shasta Abbey Press, 1987), pp. 60–63.

# *How to Sit.*

Rev. Master Jiyu-Kennett, M.O.B.C., Abbess

When sitting, one should take care that one's spine follows the natural curvature of a healthy spine, as seen in any good medical book, as much as possible. It is very important for a person learning to sit to get this right. What happens with the feet is not important; what happens to one's spine is of the utmost importance. If the spine is not correct for the individual concerned, stiffness, pain and perhaps even hallucinations may result. The weight of the body is carried easily by the lower back muscles if this position is correct; one does tend, however, to develop something of a bulge in the front, popularly called a "Zazen pot." This cannot be helped and should not be worried about. It sometimes happens that a person may have had a back injury of some sort during his or her earlier years and this may make sitting with a spine exactly right extraordinarily difficult. You should know that what we are attempting to do is to find the place where a person can sit best so as to have the very best results possible.

One never sits completely back upon the cushion or chair. When sitting on the floor, only the tip of the base of the spine should actually be on the cushion itself so that there is a slight slope from the buttocks, just seated on the edge of the cushion, to the floor where the knees rest comfortably. This posture prevents anything from pressing upon the thighs which may restrict the blood flow. If one sits fully upon the cushion, without allowing this free space for the thighs, it will be impossible to move from the cushion

This article is taken from a lecture by Rev. Master Jiyu-Kennett.

without considerable pain at a later date. The head should feel naturally comfortable and weightless upon the shoulders, with the ears in line with the latter and the nose in line with the navel. No two people are exactly the same physically so it is very important to experiment carefully for yourself so that you can be certain that you have found the right place for your head and the right place for your feet. If your ears are not exactly in line with your shoulders as a result of a back injury of some sort, do not feel that you cannot meditate. Find that place in which you are most comfortable, i.e. the place where you are most weightless, and commence your meditation in that position. One sways one's body from left to right, after the correct sitting position has been achieved, starting with large sways and ending with smaller and smaller ones; one can do circular swaying instead of this if one wishes. These types of movement enable a person to find the best position of rest for him or her as an individual; the place at which all his or her weight seems to drop straight down the spine and into the cushion or onto the chair.

The hands must not be pushed together but held in the lap with the thumbs lightly touching the ends of each other as in the illustration [on page 25]. A left-handed person places the right hand over the left, and a right-handed person the left hand over the right, for the following reason:– one side of the body is always slightly more active than the other, usually the side that one uses most, therefore, during seated meditation, one puts the hand of the less active side over the hand of the more active one since it is believed that this helps to equate the unevenness of the body's activity.

No one should ever close their eyes completely. They should be lowered so that they rest upon a spot on the floor that the meditator can see comfortably. No two people are ever comfortable at exactly the same distance of focus, therefore, although it is customary to say that it is best to allow the eyes to rest upon the floor at a distance of about one metre, it should be understood that this is not a hard and fast rule. Neither a short-sighted nor a long-sighted person could achieve this. One does not sit in meditation to do that which is unnatural for oneself, therefore, if it is normal for a person to wear spectacles, he should continue to do so whilst meditating; he should not remove them. The natural inheritance and right of all of us is to know our True Selves, that is, to be peaceful and at one with the Eternal; in order to achieve this we must not do something that is <u>unnatural</u> for <u>us</u>, as individuals, simply because meditation instructions that have been written for the perfect body say that we should.

*Question:–* I am near-sighted, should I still wear my spectacles?

*Answer:–* As I have just said, it is important that your eyes shall be able to focus <u>normally</u> and <u>naturally</u> on a spot that is comfortable. If a person is facing a wall which is, at most, six feet or so away from him, and happens to be near-sighted, he may not <u>need</u> to wear his spectacles; if he is far-sighted he probably <u>will</u> need them.

*Question:–* What should I look at?

*Answer:–* It is important to do much the same thing with the eyes that one does with one's mind. One must neither try to see anything specific, such as the patterns on the wall or floor, nor try to make such things blurry and indistinct. One should simply keep the eyes downcast and in focus. One keeps one's eyes open so as to be able to stay awake and alert. A person is not <u>trying</u> to see and, at the same time, he is not trying not to see.

It is important to breathe through the nose and not through the mouth. This is achieved quite simply by keeping the mouth shut and nothing more. It is not a hard, tight shutting that may cause the teeth to grind; it is just a simple, comfortable closing of the mouth.

When breathing, a person must not do anything that is unnatural. There are many and varied forms of so-called meditation, all of which give varying degrees of spiritual comfort. There is no form that gives greater spiritual comfort, and deeper understanding and awareness, than serene reflection meditation as far as I am concerned; however, these benefits can only be achieved if one breathes naturally. It is important to synchronise one's breathing with the natural state of one's own body. If the breathing is rough, i.e. strained or made unusual by the individual concerned, there can be no harmonisation whatsoever of body and mind. Some of us breathe more quickly than others, others more slowly. Each person must breathe in his or her own normal, natural rhythm so that no unusual stresses or strains are caused. Again, the accent is on not being unnatural.

One must not deliberately try to think nor deliberately try not to think. Thoughts come and go in our heads and we can either play with them or just sit there and allow them to pass. Too many of us allow ourselves to be hijacked by our thoughts whilst some try to deliberately push them away; both of these activities are completely incorrect. The Japanese distinguish between deliberate thought and natural thought. There is absolutely nothing wrong with natural thought. Because our ears are not plugged up during meditation, it is normal for us to hear cars passing on the roads and birds singing; because our eyes are not closed, it is only reasonable that we will notice patterns on the carpet, floor or wall: these things will only disturb us if we permit ourselves to discuss them in our own minds. If one merely notices that a car is going by there will be no problem however, if one notices that a car is going by and becomes annoyed or pleased about it, then meditation has already ceased. All that is required in meditation is that one sit with a positive attitude of mind, knowing that, if one does so, one will indeed find the True Buddha within oneself.

I have often used the example of sitting under a bridge to illustrate the above. One sits beneath a bridge across which traffic is travelling in both directions. One does not climb upon the bridge to hitch a ride in one of the cars, nor does one chase after them; one also makes no attempt to push the cars off the bridge. One cannot ignore that the cars are there; one does not have to be bothered by them. If a person does get caught by his or her thoughts which, in the beginning, is quite likely, it is important not to worry about it. One merely accepts the fact that one was caught and continues to sit, without worrying about the fact that one was caught or being guilty about it. No matter what one does, one cannot <u>change</u> the fact that one was caught and, if one worries about it, one just does not become peaceful enough to return to meditation. One should avoid guilt at all costs concerning this; there is nothing so destructive as guilt in this regard.

When the meditation is over, one sways the body from side to side or in a circular motion, exactly as one did at the beginning, except that one commences with small sways and ends with large ones.

It is important not to wear anything that is either tight or constricting. It is equally important to dress adequately so that one is neither too hot nor too cold. Great Master Dōgen, when speaking of excesses, i.e. too much warmth, too much clothing, too much food, not enough warmth, not enough clothing, not enough food, makes the following comment:– "Six parts of a full stomach support the man, the other two support his doctor." One must make sure that one is adequately fed and clothed, with just the right amount of rest, and thereafter not indulge oneself. Great Master Dōgen gives a very important warning concerning what he calls the three lacks, i.e. lack of sleep, lack of food and lack of warmth. Unless these three are exactly right, neither too much nor too little of any, the harmonisation of body and mind is impossible.

*Question:–* What happens if a person is halfway through a meditation period and cannot continue to hold the same sitting position?

*Answer:–* It is advisable to move and not worry about doing so. Seated meditation is not an endurance test. If a person feels that he or she cannot maintain the meditation position, there is nothing whatsoever wrong with changing it. Should it become necessary to move, it is very important to remember that the spine shall again be correctly aligned. It is also important to discipline oneself to a certain extent. I have always maintained that a person who feels that he can sit for ten minutes should push himself to sit for twelve minutes and that, when he is able to sit for twelve minutes, he should push himself to sit for fourteen minutes. He should continue in this way until he can maintain the same position during the full forty-five-minute sitting period without discomfort. By such means the body is disciplined gently and naturally whilst recognising that it has rights. If it is not done in this way, sitting may become something that is dreaded; I know of nothing worse than this.

*Question:–* What about fidgeting?

*Answer:–* If a person wishes to progress in meditation, it is very important for him or her to learn to sit still. Fidgeting, if the body is not uncomfortable, is a sign of a person's dislike of discipline and is a measure of the ego that is, as yet, unconverted. The debate of the opposites in our minds is not always as clearcut as we think, and the urge to fidget is sometimes a reaction to our unwillingness to do something about ourselves. If a person finds himself suffering from the urge to fidget, he should take two or three deep breaths and again realign his body since he will probably have become tense and stiff in the shoulders.

If we were all short, fat, thin or tall, had exactly the same eyesight or were in exactly the same state of health, it would be extraordinarily easy to teach meditation. However, each one of us is totally different, and this means that it is impossible to write a chapter on the mode of physical sitting necessary for meditation which will be exactly the same for everyone. It is important for a person to have himself or herself checked carefully by a competent teacher to find what is exactly the right position for him or her as an individual. Too many people try to keep the letter of the physical *Rules for Meditation* without realising that the purpose of them is to help them learn to meditate, not to cause them physical pain and unnatural discomfort.

* * *

# *Concerning the Correct Use of the Sword of Buddha's Wisdom.*

Rev. Master Jiyu-Kennett, M.O.B.C., Abbess

*[The Sword of Buddha's Wisdom or "awakening stick" is a flat wooden stick carried during meditation periods in some meditation halls. Because it has been widely misunderstood and misused in both the East and the West, the following article has been written.]*

If people, when meditating, have correctly set up the back-flowing method of breathing,[1] they may find that their shoulders have become extraordinarily tense. This is because correct breathing brings energy up the back of the body and down the front of the body and, if the person has so-called 'mental blocks,' tension develops around the shoulders. The energy that correct breathing circulates around the body gets trapped in the shoulder blades which seem to be the place where one "holds on," as it were, to private opinions, emotions, ideas, concepts, fears, worries, facades, etc. For a long time I could not understand, when in the East, why the Sword of Buddha's Wisdom was regarded as a 'massage stick'; but remember that the purpose of massage is to relieve tensions. If the awakening stick is used correctly to relieve the tensions that result from a person's energy in this area being blocked and unable to pass freely up the spine, over the head and down the sternum then it is of great value. It can relieve these blocks, at least temporarily and sometimes permanently, so that the energy may pass freely and the meditation may be full and adequate.

The awakening stick, like acupuncture and moxa burning,[2] acts as a catalyst for the removal of tensions at a time when someone least needs tension for there is no way in which a person can meditate adequately unless the energy can pass freely throughout his body. Man is body and mind and the purpose of meditation is the harmonisation of body and mind. If there is tension then the vital energy cannot move freely and the peace and beauty of true meditation cannot be known.

The Sword of Buddha's Wisdom should never be used to punish; it should never be used indiscriminately because it is thought of as something that is 'traditional'. It has a specific function and a specific purpose which I have described herein; any other use of it is a prostitution. When people feel that their shoulders are tense, as do many executives and others, they should consider well what is going on in their bodies for this is a sign that they are becoming more and more tense as a result of stress and strain and, therefore, need meditation far more than perhaps they realise. The awakening stick can relieve these tensions if they block the meditation but it can do nothing more. He who experiences pleasure from the awakening stick is wrong; he who experiences pain is wrong. Understand its use and, if you feel tense in your shoulders, ask for it. At Shasta Abbey it is never used without a request.

In the East it is used, in addition to the above occasions, to help a trainee to have the courage to become the "One Who leaps beyond all fear" (see *The Litany of the Great Compassionate One*[3]) by transcending the opposites. However, few indeed are there who know how to use it in this way.

* * *

*Notes.*

1. See Rev. Master Jiyu-Kennett's detailed explanation of correct breathing during seated meditation in the article entitled "Commentary on Dōgen's *Rules for Meditation.*"
2. The old Chinese and Japanese practice of applying heat to relieve tense muscles.
3. Rev. Master P.T.N.H. Jiyu-Kennett, M.O.B.C., *The Liturgy of the Order of Buddhist Contemplatives for the Laity* (Mt. Shasta, California: Shasta Abbey Press, 1987), pp. 84–86.

# *Serene Reflection.*

Rev. Kōten Benson, M.O.B.C.

The term *serene reflection* has been in general use since the time of Great Master Wanshi Shōkaku, 1091–1157,[1] to describe the original meditation practice of the Ch'an (Zen) tradition,[2] in contrast to the *introspecting the kōan* (C: *k'ang hua*; J: *kanna-zen*) method that was then becoming popular through the teaching of the master Daie, 1089–1163.[3]

"Serene reflection" is a translation of two Chinese characters, *mo* (J: *moku*) and *chao* (J: *shō*). A study of these characters and the levels of meaning within them may be of help to us in understanding more about our practice. I am by no means an expert in the Chinese language so I have made use of several dictionaries, books of character analysis and commentaries on the term itself to put together this article and ask forgiveness for its shortcomings.

The first character, *mo,* has an element in it that means black or darkness, making the whole character signify "dark, secret, silent, serene, profound" and also "to close the lips, to become silent".

The second character, *chao,* has as element meaning "the brightness of the sun". The whole character translates as "to reflect light, to shine on, to illume or enlighten", as well as "to reflect upon, to look upon, to have insight into".

Reprinted from *The Journal of the Order of Buddhist Comtemplatives,* vol. 4, no. 1: 33–35.

The whole term thus becomes "serene reflection", "silent illumination"[4] or "luminescent darkness".[5] In the very description of our practice we have the 'light in darkness—darkness in light' spoken of in the works of the great masters of our tradition.[6]

We can also see in this the origin of the references to the reflection of the moon in water. As the water of the spirit within us becomes still, clean and bright through meditation, so does the reflection of the "moon", of the Eternal, become clear and True. There is more than "stillness" in this, more than mere quietism. The water must be clear and bright and clean or there will only be the false "stillness" of stagnation, a dirty pool in which the moon's reflection will be dim and shallow. This is why we are warned about the consequences of clinging to blissful states and urged to maintain a bright mind while meditating—the importance of the 'stillness within activity and activity within stillness'.

Another important point in the characters is that there is no "thing" that can be grasped as the source of the light nor a "thing" that reflects the shining. Neither is the darkness or silence a "thing" that can be grasped. This is because in the face-to-face encounter with the Eternal of meditation there is no separate self, just the serene, profound, illuminating light.

Dōgen says it better than I:

> Lament impurity.
>     Within the silent waters of the heart
> Dwells the moon, the lonely waves—
>     Brightness everywhere.[7]

* * *

*Notes.*

1. Hung Chih Cheng Chueh, disciple of Tanka Shijun, author of *Mo Chao Ming (Notes on Serene Reflection).*
2. Chang, *The Practice of Zen,* pp. 66–69.
3. Ta Hui Tsung Kao (J: Daie Sōkō).
4. Another translation of *mo chao.*
5. See Rev. P.T.N.H. Jiyu-Kennett, Rōshi, *How to Grow a Lotus Blossom or How a Zen Buddhist Prepares for Death* (Mount Shasta, California: Shasta Abbey, 1977), p. 181.
6. See *Hsin Hsin Ming (Faith in Mind)* by Kanchi Sōsan; *Ts'an T'ung Ch'i (Sandōkai)* by Sekitō Kisen; *Pao Ching San Mei Ko (The Most Excellent Mirror–Samādhi)* by Tōzan Ryōkai; *Mo Chao Ming (Notes on Serene Reflection)* by Wanshi Shōkaku; "Kō Myō" ("Divine Light"), chapter 13 of *Shōbōgenzō* by Dōgen; *Kōmyōzō-Zanmai (Samādhi of the Treasury of the Radiant Light)* by Kōun Ejō and many other works in various translations.
7. See *The Story of Rev. Dōgen,* translated from the Japanese by Rev. P.T.N.H. Jiyu-Kennett.

*Bibliography.*


1. Chang, Garma C.C. *The Practice of Zen.* New York: Harper and Row, 1959.
2. Kodera, Takashi. *Dogen's Formative Years in China.* Boulder, Colorado: Prajñā Press, 1980.
3. Mathews, R. H. *Mathews' Chinese English Dictionary.* Cambridge, Massachusetts: Harvard University Press, 1948.
4. Okumura, Shōhaku. *Shikantaza: An Introduction to Zazen.* Kyoto, Japan: Kyoto Sōtō Zen Center, 1985
5. Sheng-Yen, Master. *The Poetry of Enlightenment: Poems by Ancient Ch'an Masters.* Elmhurst, New York: Dharma Drum Publications, 1987.
6. Soothill, William Edward and Lewis Hodous. *A Dictionary of Chinese Buddhist Terms.* Taipei, Taiwan: Buddhist Cultural Service.

and various and sundry dictionaries, footnotes, hints, etc., in many books.

# *Physical Postures for Meditation.*

Rev. Daishin Morgan, M.O.B.C.

By expressing the mind of meditation with your body, you bring both body and mind together in their true unity. The mind needs to be bright and alert so you should sit up straight, but without tension. The spine should have a gentle forward curve in the lumbar region so the torso can be erect, but without strain. To become familiar with the correct position of the torso, stand up straight with your feet together and relax your shoulders and abdomen. Place your forearms in the small of your back and feel how it is possible in this position to relax and yet be standing up straight. There is stability and an immovable quality that has strength without force or hardness. Notice how your hips are rotated forwards in a way that keeps the small of your back curved inwards and allows your abdomen—when it is relaxed—to hang forward.

Next, sit on a chair, preferably a dining chair or piano stool with a flat or nearly flat seat. Arrange a flattish cushion towards the back of the seat and sit down so that the base of your spine is on the cushion. (Make sure the edge of the chair does not press into your thighs.) This, in effect, gives the chair a slight forward tilt which lets the hips rotate forwards as they did when you were standing up straight as described above; your spine will then naturally go into the correctly curved position. Place your forearms in the small of your back again to make sure it feels the same as it did when you were standing straight. Unless you have a back problem that prevents you from sitting straight, do not use the back of the chair for support. Ideally your legs and feet should be together, but some people may find it difficult to relax the leg muscles unless the feet are slightly apart and the knees together.

*Meditation on a chair.*

Put your right hand on your lap with your left hand on top (or vice versa if you are left-handed) and put your thumbs together as shown in one of the photographs below. As the meditation period continues, if you become distracted your thumbs will often droop or lose contact with each other as fantasies occupy the mind. If this should happen, you can bring yourself back to the mind of meditation by simply correcting your hand position and posture.

Do not close your eyes as this encourages sleepiness and foggy states of mind; you should keep them open but lowered so that you are looking at a point on the floor or wall roughly three to six feet in front of you. Keep your eyes in focus, but do not pick on one little spot and stare at it. In a sense, you want to keep your eyes in focus but, at the same time, look within. In other words, do not get caught up in what is in front of you; allow your attention to be on the stillness. Blink naturally so that your eyes are under no strain. If you normally wear glasses, keep them on during meditation. Keep your mouth closed with your tongue touching the back of your top teeth; breathe quietly through your nose. Try to breathe naturally using both chest and abdomen so that the breath is deep and quiet, but not exaggerated. The essence of serene reflection meditation is that it is a natural activity that should be done without strain. If you notice you are breathing particularly shallowly, as often happens during periods of anxiety, then deliberately breathe more fully for a minute or two, and then go back to just sitting still. You should not get caught up with physical sensations any more than with thoughts. Although there are physical characteristics of deep meditation, you do not want to try to imitate them—just concentrate on sitting still as outlined and your body will naturally express this stillness in a way that is right for you. Everyone's body is slightly different so please remember that what is described here is a blueprint, not an absolute standard.

Another position is the kneeling posture with a meditation bench. The bench has a forward-sloping seat that supports the buttocks and prevents the ankles from being crushed or the knees being strained. The legs of the bench should only be long enough to allow the ankles to fit underneath the seat. Too high a bench, or one with too steep an angle, exaggerates the curve of the lower back and causes pain.

*Meditation on a bench.*

For those who can manage it, the cross-legged postures also provide stable positions for meditation. However, enlightenment does not depend upon sitting cross-legged so do not force yourself into painful positions and end up damaging your knees, hips or back. Approach these positions with care, only using them if they do not cause physical problems and remember that your body is the body of the Buddha and should be respected. All cross-legged positions require a meditation cushion; however, a folded blanket or pillow can be used to experiment with. Whatever you use should provide a firm base to support the tip of your spine about three to five inches off the floor. Only the tip of the spine should rest on the cushion; otherwise the cushion will press into the back of the thighs and cut off circulation.

*Meditation on a cushion.*

*Meditation in the Burmese position.*

For the Burmese position place one foot directly in front of you, the bottom of the foot touching the bottom of the opposite thigh and your other foot directly in front of the first. As with all cross-legged positions you will feel very unstable unless you have both knees on the ground, but it may take a little while for the sinews to stretch sufficiently to allow this to happen. Go carefully and do not force your knees down. This is probably the easiest cross-legged position to get into but it may require some muscular effort to hold the back in the correct position. For those with long legs this position can cause strain on the knees, so use with care.

*Trainee in the half-lotus position holding a Scripture book.*

To sit in the half-lotus position, place one foot in front of you, the bottom of the foot touching the bottom of the opposite thigh and the other foot on the opposite thigh. In the full-lotus position each foot is placed on the opposite thigh. All cross-legged positions cause a slight twist in the spine so it is very important to alternate which leg you have in front to avoid back trouble that otherwise could develop in the future. Most people find it takes a few months before they can sit cross-legged comfortably and without pain for a full meditation period of thirty minutes. At the outset, gradually ease yourself into the position shown and sit for a short time. If you want to try sitting cross-legged, it is essential to get your posture checked at a meditation group meeting, or at one of our priories or retreats before too long.

*Meditation in the full-lotus position.*

When more than one period of seated meditation (which should not be more than forty-five minutes), are scheduled, they are alternated with periods of walking meditation. Each forty-five minute period of seated meditation is followed ideally by a fifteen-minute period of walking meditation: sitting without such movement for longer periods can cause serious physical injury to the feet, knees, hips and back. This is true for all of the postures described above. Walking meditation also helps us to appreciate that meditation is not dependent on physical immobility: it can be a bridge between formal meditation and meditation within the activities of daily life. It can also be usefully practised if sleepiness becomes a persistent problem.

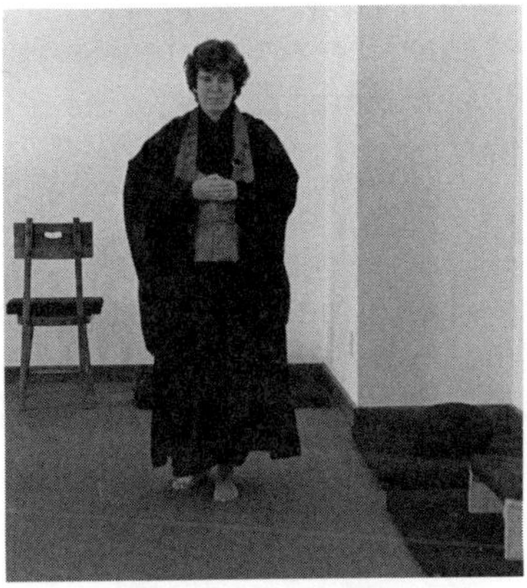

*Walking meditation.*

> Get up slowly and gently and commence to do your kinhin. Kinhin *[walking meditation]* is done by making a fist of the left hand, with the thumb inside, and covering it with the right hand; it should not be held tightly against the chest wall but in an oval position. The arms, being held loosely, form an oval at the level of the chest with the elbows extended. The body must always be erect with the eyes again still in their naturally lowered position, not closed nor looking too far ahead of the feet....Beginning with the left foot, walk calmly and slowly, with great dignity; do not walk absent-mindedly; a step of not more than six inches at a time should be taken. Walk first on the

> heel and then along the side of the foot ending upon the toes so that the foot digs itself into the ground as it were. This is done for five to ten minutes after each period of thirty or forty minutes sitting. Remember that this is moving Zazen; it is not done *[merely]* for the purpose of stretching the legs as some people think.[1]

In exactly the same way as when sitting, you just sit, so when walking, just walk. If the mind wanders off, then patiently bring it back to just walking. In this way, mind and body become one and we are able to realise our true nature.

Meditation can also be done whilst lying down, although this position should only be used when illness or disability prevents one from sitting up. The best position is to lie flat on your back with feet together and hands clasped at the chest in the same position as described for walking meditation, except that the hands are allowed to rest against the chest. Some people find it helpful to slowly move their feet to help keep awake, and others find it necessary to have their knees slightly raised. Keep your eyes open in a position that corresponds to a downward gaze if you were sitting up.

Once the sitting practice is over, you then get up and attend to whatever needs to be done, doing it with the mind of meditation. If your mind wanders off, you quietly bring it back to the job in hand so that work becomes meditation in exactly the same way as sitting becomes meditation. It is easiest to learn how to make work into meditation with simple, manual activities like walking up and down stairs, washing up, using the lavatory, cleaning the house, etc. Whenever fantasy takes over, recognise what is happening, let go of it, and come back to what you are doing. In time you become a lot more concentrated and this has many beneficial side-effects as you learn to bring the mind of meditation into all activities of life. In the end, meditation truly becomes a twenty-four-hour-a-day activity.

* * *

*Note.*

1. Rōshi P.T.N.H. Jiyu-Kennett, *Zen is Eternal Life,* 3rd ed. rev. (Mt. Shasta, California: Shasta Abbey Press, 1987), pp. 31–32.

*Purify your own heart and penetrate the depths of yourself through meditation. Then you will see all things clearly, obscured by nothing. Therefore we say that there is no mountain barrier and no river separation. The bright light penetrates every corner of the world.*

*Great Master*
*Wanshi Shōkaku.*

# *The Mind of Meditation.*

Rev. Daishin Morgan, M.O.B.C.

Serene reflection is a method of meditation that can be summarized as 'just sitting'. To just sit still is the simplest of all activities and yet within it we obstruct ourselves with all manner of unnecessary complexities. The essence of serene reflection meditation is to simply *be* without adding anything or taking anything away. It is based on the fundamental teaching of the Mahayana tradition that the Buddha Nature is the foundation of our being. The Buddha Nature is the source of all compassion, love, and wisdom. It is the place from which real love flows out to all without distinguishing one from another. It is this love we all seek, for the ability to give and receive this love is the ability to know perfection, it is the experience of true peace.

The Buddha Nature is not something that exists inside of us like a soul, nor is it something external and apart from us like a god. It is all of existence for it rejects nothing. Infinite compassion, love, and wisdom are the characteristics by which we recognise it but it also embraces what we regard as negative within ourselves and the world around us. The Buddha Nature is enlightenment itself and since it embraces all of existence it includes us. We are not separate from enlightenment but we have mistaken where our true refuge lies. Instead of trusting the Buddha Nature, that which is in tunc with all of existence, we take refuge in an illusory sense of self, a self that is fundamentally at war with all of existence. Serene reflection meditation is the means we have of healing the rift we have created between ourselves and the Buddha Nature. Enlightenment is inherent within every one of us, but to know that enlightenment we have to look towards it for our refuge and cease to involve ourselves with greed, hate, and delusion.

Buddha Nature is the essence of stillness; it appears whenever we neither reject nor hang on to anything. To do serene reflection meditation means that you accept everything that arises in stillness, without judgement and without excuse. You must be still with whatever arises in all its exposed and revealed nature. This is to learn how to see without preconceptions. Meditation is the means we have of coming to know and experience for ourselves that which is true and real. This experience must be direct; that is, it must not take place through filters of past conditioning. If anger arises in meditation we learn to be still with it and simply accept that anger has arisen. We add nothing to it by continuing a series of thoughts about the incident which caused us to get angry, indulging a running commentary justifying our position, going over what we will say next time we meet the person who made us angry, and so on and on. Equally, we do not try to pretend we are not angry by refusing to look at what is actually happening. The way to meditate when anger arises is to sit there and be willing to be angry without judging ourselves as bad or unworthy, and without indulging the anger by carrying on the mental jabbering.

To illustrate this I will describe how it feels to come to terms with anger in myself. Having settled myself down to formal seated meditation, a memory from the past comes to mind of a particular incident that made a deep impression on me. There is a lot of anger associated with this memory and, as I find myself getting involved in the apparently inevitable commentary that always seems to accompany the memory, I become aware that I am involved in a never-ending cycle of thought that just keeps going round and round. I then deliberately let go of the thought process and each time the mind returns to it I simply say to myself quietly and firmly: No, I do not want this, I wish to be still. Since meditation is not a state of vacuity, when I let go of the thoughts I start to become more aware of the underlying feelings. By letting go of the commentary, I start to feel first hand what is actually happening. I become aware of a sense of outrage. To keep the meditation going I must not judge or excuse this, but simply be willing to know the outrage that exists at that moment. This, put another way, means I allow the outrage to be enfolded in the stillness. Complete acceptance is the hallmark of love; it is there within love that the outrage is embraced. I can now see that the outrage is covering a deep sense of hurt and grief. To continue meditating, I must allow the grief to arise and be still within it, allowing this, too, to be embraced within the loving acceptance that is the stillness. I then become aware, not in words but by simply seeing it unfolding, that behind the hurt and grief lies a fear that I am inadequate and in some fundamental way will never measure up. Again this knowledge is not to be falsely anaesthetised by justification, or by rushing off to prove it is not true by desperately seeking some external worth in the eyes of others. Instead, just as before, this deep sense of inadequacy must be embraced; I must sit there and feel inadequate without running away. When I do this something quite remarkable then takes place. I realise that there is something beneath the inadequacy, I begin to see there is something infinitely still and accepting that embraces all of this—I cannot say it is me, I cannot say it is not me—it is just that when I am still all that arises is embraced within a great loving acceptance. I am embraced within it, it is all of me and there is nothing inadequate, there never has been, and there never will be.

This is what it means to just sit still. When this is done the anger I started with has led me directly to the Eternal Buddha, the Buddha Nature. Thus I begin to understand how it is that there is nothing outside the Eternal Buddha, even that which at first sight seems negative. Indeed, all things point to the Truth when they are looked at with the eye of meditation.

There is not necessarily a strong and powerful memory that comes to mind every time you sit down for formal meditation. Many people experience longish periods where nothing very much seems to happen. Some people even sit for years and years waiting for something to happen and it never seems to. This is a condition in which one needs to learn to look deeper at what is going on. There is always plenty happening within meditation but we have to learn how to see it.

I mentioned earlier the importance of having the body in an alert position. This is because mind and body are not separate things; if the body is alert it helps to keep the mind bright. In a similar kind of way all the layers of delusion we get involved in give rise to corresponding tensions within the body. Very often these tensions, or some of them at least, become apparent in the abdomen area. When you take up your sitting position you need to relax your abdomen, let your stomach hang out. When we try to achieve this relaxed posture we become aware of tensions in this area. We are unable to just relax; there is a bit of a knot in there we do not seem able to let go of. For many people it can seem as though there is a whole web of tensions preventing the abdomen from returning to its naturally relaxed position. If you start to get all worried about these tensions you only add to them. They come about because we constantly try to present an image to ourselves and to the world that is not accurate. We feel our self-respect depends upon the maintenance of this image and so we are very afraid of letting it go. The way forward is to just be aware that the tensions exist, and, as it were, cradle them within the loving acceptance I spoke of earlier. If you have your hands in the recommended position for formal meditation they are at the level of or below the navel; your arms surround the abdomen and all its tensions and it is as though your arms are the all-embracing arms of the Buddha Nature. Just be still within this loving acceptance and do not try to make the tensions go away—that is to go on playing the same old game. Just be still and embrace the tension, being willing for it to be there. When you do this you find that the tensions begin to unlock; you begin to see directly what causes them without a lot of discursive thought. I must stress that this is not analysis but looking directly, embracing. You will begin to see what the causes are but you may not be able to put them into words. That does not matter in the least—what matters is that you unlock the tensions.

Just as happened with the anger, so in this case the tension itself reveals to us what lies beneath it. When we touch, or rather when we are touched by the Eternal, then we know that a refuge exists that is beyond any image. It is a true refuge that nothing can destroy. The beauty of it is that we find the refuge by means of what, at first sight, is the very obstacle that keeps us from it! Whatever arises within meditation, be it the sense of great compassion or boiling hate, by simply being still and not indulging it, we are lead by it directly to the Eternal. There are no real obstacles provided we keep meditating. There is no substitute for practice where meditation is concerned; you come to understand what it is and how it works by doing it, and by doing it regularly.

The result of doing meditation is that you become aware of many things in your life that need to be changed. If you wish to go deeper with your practice, then those changes will need to be made. There is no limit to how far the practice goes and in the end we have to give up everything. I do not mean we must rush out and give away all we possess—it is actually much harder than that. You have, in the end, to come to a place where you go beyond all you have known in the past. Some people experience this in meditation as approaching a cliff edge which you know you need to step over, but you cannot see if there is anything there to hold you. Most of us turn tail at this point and hide. It is important then not to condemn ourselves, but accept the fear within the same loving acceptance. We then find ourselves returning to that cliff edge and maybe we turn and run again, but in time we approach it, and, almost before we realise what has happened, we step off; we let go of all that we believe ourselves to be and trust the Eternal absolutely. We then find we are within the hand of the Eternal Buddha and always were. What we have had to give up is the clinging to the idea that we are separate. Once we know we are in the hand of the Eternal, there is an end to fear. If life comes, there is life; if death comes, there is death: we are free to live fully and freely without the tyranny of fear. I have yet to meet someone who was able to take this leap without having a few 'trial runs' at the first. We all have within us what it takes to train, we lack for nothing, but it takes time to grow the necessary faith in ourselves and the Eternal. All we need for the great work is at hand; meditation is the means we have of discovering it.

Some people worry that meditation is a way of hiding from the world, but, on the contrary, through coming to understand one's true relationship with the Eternal Buddha and all beings, you begin to see more clearly where your resposibilities lie. Meditation is not an antisocial activity, quite the reverse; it is the still point of certainty, the source of strength that enables one to act with compassion and wisdom, which are unfettered by fear. However, one's practice should not become obsessive; a sense of humour should be maintained whilst still understanding the great seriousness of the work. Most people have so many commitments that there is little chance of their practice becoming obsessive, but in these days of unemployment some may find themselves with a great deal of time on their hands.

Meditation is a very valuable use of this time, but remember that meditation is for oneself and for all beings as well. One needs to give in practical forms expression to the compassion that arises in meditation. It is not a good idea to spend hours and hours doing one's own practice in isolation from the rest of the world. This can lead one to lose perspective on reality. Remember to maintain a balance between formal meditation and practical meditation (meditation in action). Even monks living in a monastery do not spend their whole day doing formal meditation, and much time is spent in practical activities that benefit others.

* * *

# *Obstacles in Meditation Practice.*

Rev. Kōshin Schomberg, M.O.B.C.

In the *Scripture of Great Wisdom* (the *Heart Sutra*), which is the essential scripture of the meditation schools of Buddhism, there is the statement that the spiritual obstacles in the mind of the Bodhisattva dissolve through oneness with Great Wisdom. It is important to know that there is no spiritual obstacle that will not eventually dissolve if one continues one's training. This is an essential element of a Buddhist's faith. With this in mind, I would like to discuss briefly a few commonly encountered difficulties in the hope of assisting people who are beginning serene reflection meditation training.

*Irregular Meditation Practice.* Just as our negative habits are strengthened through repetition, and especially through regular repetition, the habit of bright acceptance—the attitude of serene reflection meditation—is strengthened through repetition, especially *regular* repetition. A persistent difficulty in establishing a regular practice of sitting meditation may be indicative of an underlying fear. It can be very helpful in dealing with this difficulty to establish regular meditation periods—for example, once daily, morning or evening—in which one sits for only a very short time. Even a few minutes is sufficient in the beginning. The short duration of the meditation period will help relax the fear gently and gradually. Regularity is far more important than duration of sitting periods, though with time one will want to sit for a longer period. Every time one sits down to meditate, one is beckoning to the Eternal Buddha Nature. In doing this regularly, we develop the habit of opening the heart to the Eternal and this habit gradually pervades and transforms our entire life. The key here is to push gently against the resistance through regular practice. Then, once a week or so, one can set a day aside in which one does not do formal meditation. (Some people find that they end up doing some that day just for the pure enjoyment of it, but it is important that there be no sense of obligation or necessity. This rest day helps invigorate a long-term practice.)

*Striving*. This often is just the reverse side of the reluctance that makes regular practice difficult. Striving is a well-intentioned but somewhat misguided effort. It involves pushing oneself too hard by sitting too frequently or too long. For most people, formal meditation done once or twice each day (with a day of rest or renewal as mentioned above each week or so) is adequate as the basis of daily practice. Of course, one cannot make a general rule since people differ greatly, but it can be said that when striving is present the effort is heavy and desperate. As said above, *regular* practice is the essential thing. It is enough to respectfully and regularly knock at the gates of enlightenment: it is not necessary to try to pound them in.

*One-sided Views on Meditation and Training*. In fifteen years as a monk, I have come to the point where I not only do not know what will, or will not, happen next, but I can be sure that if I cared to speculate on the subject I would be wrong. It is amazing how quickly our theories come to the aid of our desires—and how mistaken both can be. In doing meditation and training, a naïve and humble attitude of mind is very helpful. The spiritual life is full of inexhaustible riches which are given gradually as we are ready to receive them. We cannot anticipate them, nor can we control them. We can only make ourselves receptive to them by training as sincerely as we can. In meditating, we must continually let go of what we have known and experienced in the past. For that to which we are opening ourselves in meditation is Infinite, and our little opinions are never going to be adequate in the presence of the Infinite. It is necessary to train in respect and gratitude, and, respectfully and gratefully, go beyond things we have read, old opinions and the *greed* to understand and control.

*Difficulty Accepting the Full Religious Implications of Meditation.* Many Western people come to Buddhism expecting it to be a kind of non-religious religion. And, of course, it does differ in many ways from the religions in which many of us were raised. But Buddhism *is* a religion, and it requires us to have real faith. This faith is not a matter of professed creed or belief. It is the faith that there *is* That which is a true Refuge and that we can find this Refuge through meditation and training. A person who does Buddhist practice and persists in it through all the ups and downs of life has this faith, whether he or she *knows* it or not.

The natural movement of faith is in the direction of a constant deepening. Thus it grows into the understanding and the certainty that there *is* the Eternal. Its growth is unending. Yet *we* may not always be perfectly willing for that deepening to continue. Sometimes, people try to arrest faith at a certain point in its development. This is done out of fear. One may work very hard at this "putting on the brakes," but it never works.

In Buddhism, there is the Refuge of the Buddha (meaning both the historical Buddha and the Eternal Buddha Nature). There is also the Refuge of the Dharma—the teaching of the Buddha and of our own Buddha Nature. And there is the Refuge of the Sangha—those who follow the Buddha and those who seek, long for and know the Eternal. In doing meditation, we are directly taking Refuge in the

Eternal. And if we are sincere and continue our training, we will find that we are increasingly drawn to take Refuge in the Dharma and in the Sangha. It is important to allow the natural movement of the heart toward the *Three* Refuges to flow forth unhindered. Sometimes, people want to meditate, but do not want to hear the Buddha's Teaching or train with, and seek the advice of, spiritual seniors. A great Buddhist Master said, "the Way is only difficult to those who pick and choose."[1] It is helpful, when we find ourselves putting on the brakes, to recognize that we are afraid of something and to use this as an incentive to look more deeply within our own heart for the key to a deeper trust. It is very unhelpful to get involved in one's own, or others', rationalizations and intellectual theories which always attempt to justify fears. If we remain still within our own heart and long to do the right thing, we will receive the help we need.

*The Gap between Meditation and Daily Life.* Many years ago, Rev. Master Jiyu-Kennett's Chinese ordination master visited Shasta Abbey. His name was The Very Reverend Seck Kim Seng and he visited America, as it turned out, shortly before his death. He came to see how Rev. Master was faring in America and he spoke to each of her disciples in private with just another Chinese monk present as an interpreter. When I went in to see him I was in my mid-twenties and a very new novice monk. I had no idea what he would say. He asked me, with great kindness, what I wanted in becoming a monk. The question had never occurred to me and I said the first thing that popped into my mind: "I want to be able to meditate in everything I do." I left the room thinking that I must have appeared pretty dumb: it did not seem like a very glorious or momentous spiritual ambition.

I have since realized how much more wisdom was embodied in my naïve answer to the old priest's question than in my afterthoughts. Many people feel, as I did, a considerable gap between formal meditation and the quality of daily life. People react in different ways to this seeming gulf. Some want to cling to formal meditation and this can lead to the problem of striving mentioned above. Others despair so much of imbuing their daily life with the serenity that they experience at times in meditation that they abandon practice altogether. The only answer I know to this problem is just to continue one's training in the faith that with time the seeming gap will disappear. And this is in fact what eventually happens. But I would emphasize that it does not happen at all as I vaguely thought and hoped it would. The reality is far greater than we can possibly anticipate. We can safely say that, while one may not know how the Truth will manifest within one's life, regular meditation, the study and practice of the Buddhist Precepts, the cultivation at all times and in all circumstances of an attitude of respect and gratitude, and the willing training with others and under the guidance of the best Teacher one can find provide the essential means to that unforeseeable goal.

* * *

*Note.*

1. Seng Ts'an (J: Kanchi Sōsan), "Faith in Mind." For one translation of the whole poem see Master Sheng-Yen, trans. and ed., *The Poetry of Enlightenment: Poems by Ancient Ch'an Masters* (Elmhurst, New York: Dharma Drum Publications, 1987), p. 25.

# *Possible Physical Problems Met with in Meditation.*

Peter Lavin, Lay Minister, O.B.C.

When we sit we take refuge in the Three Treasures. It is easy to see that we are taking refuge in our own Buddha nature (not that this is separate from everyone else's) but we should also remember that we take refuge in the Dharma and in the Sangha. We should be aware, too, that we need to find the middle way, the path between the opposites.

As far as the physical side of meditation is concerned, the Sangha can help us make sure that we have as correct a posture as our body allows. At the outset we should ask a priest to check the way we are sitting. If, later, problems arise we should make sure that these are not caused by our sitting improperly, and it is always good to check with a priest when any apparent difficulty arises.

We take refuge in the Dharma during meditation by listening to all the teaching that comes to us, and this includes through our body. As we begin to sit up straight in the presence of the Buddhas and Ancestors our body often complains that we are pushing it into unaccustomed shapes. Here we need to find the line between giving in too easily to discomfort and causing ourselves unnecessary pain. As a general rule we should sit still with the ache until we really have to move and then change to a comfortable position with as little fuss as possible. If, however, we find the pain persists we should seek advice from a priest or, if appropriate, a doctor.

There is no need to sit cross-legged, which usually results in aching knees and ankles if we are not used to it, but, if we do, it is essential that we alternate the position of our legs each time we sit to avoid permanent damage to the spine or hips. Generally our body will warn us if we are causing it lasting harm but this is not always the case. It is good to examine in detail why we are sitting cross-legged if that is what we choose to do.

Discomfort may also come from being too tense. This can often result in pains in the back or shoulders. Here again we need to find the balance between holding ourselves stiffly erect and sagging. Once we have straightened our backs we should relax our body but make sure our mind is still alert. The tenseness or laxity of our thumbs in the meditation mudra during meditation is a good indication of whether we are too tense or too relaxed.

If we find that our legs have gone to sleep during the meditation period, we have probably been cutting off the circulation by sitting too far back on our seat or pressing one leg on top of the other. A small cushion on the chair can raise the bottom sufficiently to prevent this. Legs that have fallen asleep buckle under the weight of standing, so to prevent winding up on the floor, always make sure that the circulation to the legs is normal *before* trying to stand. Sometimes they can fall asleep without our being aware of it.

In the beginning we may be distracted by certain physical effects. It can take a little practice to keep the eyes focussed on the wall in front of us without getting caught by patterns or shadows, or going off into a slightly trance-like unfocussed state. At times the wall may appear closer or further away than we know it is. As soon as we are aware of any of these we simply need to bring our mind back to just sitting, perhaps blink once or twice, and focus our eyes on the wall without examining it in detail. If we usually wear glasses to focus our eyes at that distance we should wear them for meditation and our eyes should be allowed to blink in the usual way; otherwise we may find they begin to water.

Drowsiness is something that can arise because we are tired or for reasons that are not so easy to understand. Sitting in a well-ventilated room that is not too hot and trying to find time for our meditation before the end of the day can help here. If we find that we are falling asleep for no apparent reason we probably need to experiment to find what works for us. Some people find that putting their hands in gasshō until the drowsiness passes helps. For others a repeated act of will may be called for (perhaps asking the help of Āchalanātha,[1] for we are never sitting alone). We may need to remind ourselves of why we have come to our sitting place and make sure our mind is bright and positive.

Meditation can only be learnt by doing it and it is a continuing process. Just as we sit and let the thoughts come and go, so can we let the physical distractions come and go: if we are sitting properly, our Buddha nature will draw our attention to those we should pay heed to, and that is when to take refuge in the Three Treasures.

* * *

*Note.*

1. Āchalanātha, the Unmoving Lord (J: Fudō-myō-ō), is one of the Guardians of the Gateways to training. He represents one aspect of the Eternal—the will to train, to sit still and be unmoved by anything within or outside of ourselves. We can call on the help of this aspect of the Eternal and find that place within each of us that is immovable, imperturbable, indestructible.

# *Your Place of Meditation.*

Rev. Shikō Rom, F.O.B.C.

*The means of training are thousandfold,*
*but pure meditation must be done.*[1]

Although meditation can be done everywhere, it is very helpful to have a place set aside in your home for doing formal meditation. In monasteries, the meditation and ceremony halls are decorated carefully and beautifully to help strengthen faith in what they represent—the beauty inherent in all existence, the Eternal (Buddha Nature) which is found within ourselves and all things. They are kept neat and clean and treated with great respect. In setting up your own sitting place, you can keep these attitudes in mind; for in doing so, you are encouraged to believe that there is something beautiful within yourself and all things, something that is worthy of care and respect.

Setting up an altar and meditation room.

Keep in mind that you want to make the place in which you do formal meditation the least distracting and most conducive to meditation as possible. The ideal is to have a quiet room in your home that is used only for meditation. If this is not possible, a part of a room that will not be used for anything else during your meditation periods—a corner of your bedroom or living room, for example—will work fine. It is not always possible to find a place that is completely quiet: you may hear traffic, a dog barking occasionally, people walking by. You can learn to meditate with a certain amount of noise; however, you want to avoid being around

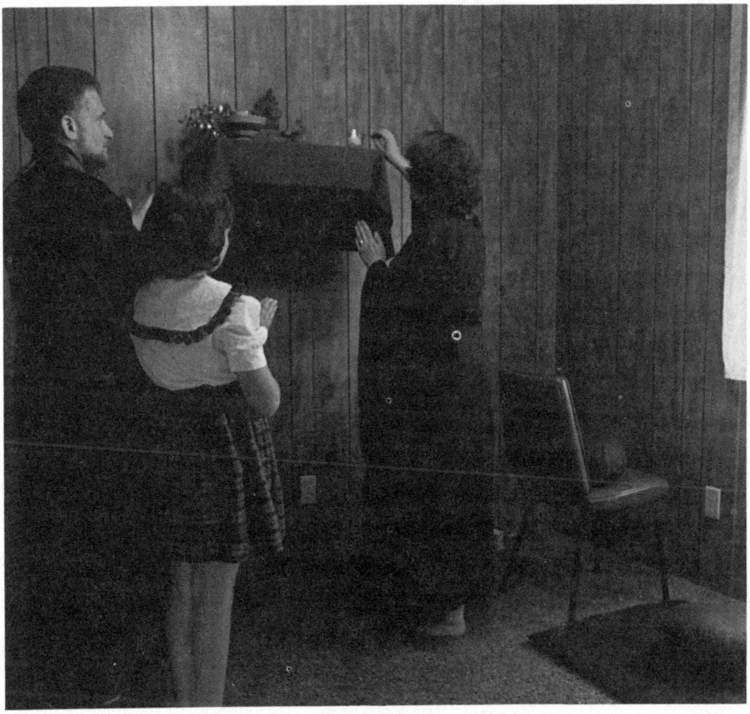

*Meditation room and home altar.*

such things as television, music or loud talking, which can be very distracting especially to someone new to meditation.

A small altar, as a reminder of the Eternal and one's purpose for training, is often placed in the meditation room or near one's sitting place. The altar itself can be a small table, a wall-mounted shelf or a specially-made altar cabinet. A statue or picture of a Buddha or some aspect of the Eternal, such as great compassion (Avalokiteshvara Bodhisattva), great love (Samantabhadra Bodhisattva) or great wisdom (Mañjushri Bodhisattva) is placed in the center at the back. To symbolize the blossoming of enlightenment, flowers are placed to the left of the statue and, out of concern for all living things, artificial flowers or potted plants are used instead of cut ones. A candle or altar light is placed on the right side, signifying the light of Eternal Wisdom. Placed directly in front of the statue or picture, a water-offering cup expresses the cleansing aspect of the Eternal. An incense burner is in front of the water-offering cup, the offering of incense representing gratitude for the Three Treasures: the Buddha (the historical Buddha, Shakyamuni, and one's own Buddha Nature), the Dharma (the teaching transmitted through Shakyamuni Buddha), and the Sangha (those who live by the Buddha's teaching). Vegetarian offerings (fresh or dried fruit, nuts, prepared food, or any food edible without cooking) may be placed on the altar as well, representing the willingness to share the benefits of training with all beings.

If you are meditating on the floor and your room is not carpeted, it is advisable to place a large flat cushion or piece of carpeting beneath your meditation cushion or bench to help prevent pains in the legs and knees. You want to have the temperature in the room within a comfortable range, preferably on the cool side. One or two windows for natural light and air circulation are good. The lighting should be gentle: during the day, light from a window will probably be sufficient; when it is dark, a candle, small lamp or altar light can be used. Meditation is an inward-looking process; for that reason we meditate facing a wall, and it should be as non-distracting as possible.

### Clothing.

Body and mind are one. Your outward appearance reflects your inward state of mind and can help or hinder your meditation. If you sit up straight, are clean and dressed neatly, you not only convey a bright, positive attitude, but you are also more likely to find that brightness and positivity. The clothing worn for meditation should be clean, respectful and comfortable. At Shasta Abbey, lay trainees change from work clothes to their meditation clothing for each meditation period: loose-fitting clothing is advisable—slacks that do not put pressure around the waist or restrict circulation when the legs are bent or a long skirt that is full enough to allow the legs to be bent underneath. Do not wear bedclothing (except when meditating as you go to sleep or when ill).

The meditation period.

Treat your sitting place with respect. At the monastery, we bow as we enter or leave the meditation hall, thus showing gratitude for having a nice place to sit. We then bow to our sitting place (cushion, bench, or chair) and turn around and bow to everyone else who is meditating with us. Once seated, we bow again to begin and end the meditation period. This helps us in many ways: when we bow we express our gratitude, and the act of bowing itself helps us to find that gratitude; it helps us bring ourselves together when we feel scattered; and it helps us bow to our Greater Selves, for it is only when we put our trust in that which is greater than ourselves, the Eternal, that we find what we are looking for. Even when sitting alone, we still bow "to others" before and after sitting, thus recognizing that we train for both ourselves and others and that we are grateful for the training of others.

Before each meditation period you can offer incense at the altar (or simply in an incense burner if you do not have an altar), blessing the incense by touching the base of the incense stick to your forehead and reciting the Three Homages aloud or to yourself ("Homage to the Buddha; Homage to the Dharma; Homage to the Sangha") before putting it into the incense burner. You may time the meditation period by the burning of the incense stick (the short stick incense that we use at Shasta Abbey burns for thirty minutes and the long stick incense burns for forty-five) or you can time it with an hour-glass or a gentle-sounding alarm clock or watch. If a few people are meditating together, usually one person times the meditation period, ringing a gong to begin and end it. After you stand up from meditation, you again bow to your seat and bow outwards to everyone else. You may also wish to recite a Scripture and offertory verse before or after a meditation period, Great Master Dōgen's *Rules for Meditation* being a very useful one.

## When to meditate.

At Shasta Abbey we sit formally when we first get up in the morning, mid-afternoon, and at eight in the evening. Rising time varies during the year: during formal monastic terms, it is usually forty-five minutes before dawn so that we are meditating during the half hour before dawn. Some people find that on first arising in the morning, especially if this is before dawn, their minds tend to be bright and positive. The Buddha Nature within us is always bright and positive; through old habits, likes, dislikes, opinions and the like, we create clouds that cover up this brightness. I have found that when I am freshly awakened from sleep in the early morning, the clouds are fewer or have not yet formed, and I am able to see the brightness and feel faith more easily. Meditation in the afternoon is an opportunity to be still once again and find our true purpose in the midst of a busy day. Meditation in the evening can help us see and let go of whatever has been happening during the day and renew our faith if events have obscured it. These times may not be possible for you: find what fits into your schedule so that you will actually be able to meditate on a regular basis; you can do seated, formal meditation any time during the day except for the forty-five minutes or so after a meal when your food is digesting.

When you first start, you may only want to sit for five or ten minutes and gradually work up to twenty or thirty minutes once or twice a day. It is better to start out slowly than to overdo it at first and then lose interest; but, try to meditate every day, if only for a few minutes, as it is important to commit yourself to a regular practice—the times when you least feel like meditating can be the times of greatest benefit. You can meditate formally once or twice a day, or more often, if you have the time, although you should not meditate for longer than forty-five minutes without a period of walking meditation and possibly a short rest. You can also take a few minutes periodically throughout the day wherever you are to bring yourself back to the stillness of meditation and get in touch again with what really matters. No matter how busy your life may seem, you can always find the time and place to meditate if you really want to.[2]

The purpose of having a special place for meditation that you care for and respect is so that you can begin to open the door to your True Self, so that you can start to find that Something that warrants great care and respect. However, the Eternal can be found everywhere and in all circumstances, and we eventually discover that the true meditation hall is within our own hearts and that we carry it with us wherever we go. The priest Nyogen Senzaki wrote:

> Like a snail I carry
> My humble Zendō[3] with me.
> It is not as small as it looks,
> For the boundless sky joins it
> When I open a window.[4]

*Notes.*

1. *Rules for Meditation.*
2. It is inadvisable to spend many hours in formal meditation to the neglect of one's responsibilities or spend hour upon hour in formal meditation on one's own, without the direction of a qualified spiritual teacher.
3. Meditation hall.
4. Quoted from *Like a Dream, Like a Fantasy: The Zen Writings and Translations of Nyogen Senzaki,* edited and with an introduction by Eido Shimano Rōshi and published in 1978.

# *Children and Meditation.*

Rev. Master Jiyu-Kennett, M.O.B.C., Abbess

I am often asked, "How do you teach meditation to children and what is the best age to start at?" In the east the average child is taught to meditate as soon as it is possible for it to sit upright; i.e. around one or two years old. No doctrine is put into the child's head. The mother and father, and the rest of the family, will sit quietly in front of the family altar; the child, without being restrained, will either sit for a few moments or roll around on the floor with the parents taking no notice. The parents thus express their knowledge of the child's latent understanding and do not treat it as less than themselves. In a very short time the child wants to sit like the parents, as do, interestingly enough, the dog and cat. I have sat down to meditate and my cat has come up, looked at the wall and then sat down to look at it with me. Thus, if the parents meditate, the child will meditate too. I have seen children at the age of two and a half doing formal meditation in the laymen's meditation hall in Sōjiji—and doing a wonderful job. I have photographs of them. These children do a meditation so pure and exquisite it is unbelievable to watch; but they would not be able to discuss the Buddha Nature with you, nor would they be able to put into words the doctrine of the Trikaya—nor would they be able to explain the "all is one" and the "all is different" that their little bodies express. Their explanations are not as the world understands explanations. And yet every

From "The Education of the Buddhist Child" by Rev. Rōshi Jiyu-Kennett; reprinted from *The Journal of Shasta Abbey,* December 1974: 12–16.

*Members of the Shasta Abbey Sunday School sitting in the guest house meditation room.*

part of their bodies will express the "all is one" and the "all is different"—they will express the Buddha Nature for they have learned to meditate with their whole being untrammelled by duality. They are indeed whole creatures and can teach us much.

* * *

# *Every-minute Meditation.*

Rev. Daizui MacPhillamy, M.O.B.C.

Most students of Buddhism know that the practice of meditation is not something which is limited to the times each day we spend in formal seated meditation. But to bring the mind of meditation out of the meditation hall and into our everyday world of work and daily living is not always an easy thing to do. I would like to share with you a method for helping to do this. It is a practice common to many schools of Buddhism and is known variously as "mindfulness training", "working meditation", or "every-minute meditation". The method can be summarized in five steps:

1. Do one thing at a time.
2. Pay attention to what you are doing.
3. When your mind wanders to something else, bring it back.
4. Repeat step number three a few hundred thousand times.
5. But, if your mind keeps wandering to the same thing over and over, stop for a minute; maybe it is trying to tell you something important.

That is all there is to it. It is incredibly simple and requires nothing more than the willingness to do it with some persistence, yet, at least for me, it has been second only to formal seated meditation as the most important method of practice in my training.

The reason for step number one is not hard to see: if we accept that Truth is One and undivided, then It can only be

Reprinted, with changes, from *The Journal of Shasta Abbey,* vol. XII, nos. 5 and 6: 18–22.

realized by a mind which is itself unified and aware. Such one-pointedness and mindfulness are, by definition, impossible when you are doing two things at once or are not paying attention to what you are doing. Thus, if you choose to try this practice, it means no more eating breakfast, talking to your spouse, and watching "Good Morning America" all at the same time; planning your ten o'clock meeting while you drive to work is out; so are thinking about skiing while you do the dishes, reading a magazine while you're on the toilet, and worrying about your finances while you plant your garden.

This practice, you will note, is exactly what the schedule, rules, and ceremonial of a training monastery help one to do. For the new trainee in a monastery, the opportunities to learn this art are considerable. He or she does so naturally if he simply follows the schedule and keeps his mind on what he is doing. The postulancy and novitiate are times in a monastic career when the method of every-minute meditation can be most easily practiced. Not all of us, however, are attracted to a monastic vocation, and even those who are so inclined do not remain beginning trainees forever. For most people, therefore, the task is a little harder because there are usually many things which we could (or, worse yet, should) be doing at any given time, and the temptation to do more than one of them is great. A person in this position may find it helpful to add a "step zero" before the first step. Step zero is to decide what is the one most important thing to be doing at this particular moment; then, do it.

Not only must we do one thing at a time, but also we must pay attention to the one thing that we are doing. This attention should be the same as that used in formal seated meditation. One must not exclude thoughts, perceptions, emotions, etc.; yet whenever one is aware of having become attached to, or enmeshed in, them, one brings one's mind back to focus on the task at hand. It is very important to understand this statement. Mindfulness training is not the same as focusing the concentration upon one object to the exclusion of all other things. That would be simply a different way to create a duality, to divide up the world. It would also be dangerous: people who exclude things from their awareness tend to deceive themselves and to have accidents. This, by the way, is one means the teachers in a Buddhist monastery have of knowing if the students are doing the practice of mindfulness correctly. If they are doing it right, they become more efficient at their jobs; if they've got it backwards, they start having accidents or become inefficient. So, you exclude nothing from awareness, but when you realize that you have become distracted, then your attention is gently returned to the present activity. This is repeated hundreds, perhaps thousands, of times a day, and there is a certain amount of trial and error involved in learning how to do it correctly.

So much for steps number one through four. They are not hard to understand; with them it is really mostly a matter of whether or not one decides to do them. Step five, however, requires more exploration. Occasionally a thought just will not leave you alone. No matter how many times you bring your mind back to the business at hand, this thought keeps insisting itself upon your consciousness. There is sometimes a good reason for this: the thought is trying to tell you something. What I do in this circumstance is to stop what I am doing and take that "bothersome" thought seriously for a moment. In other words, I make thinking about that topic the one thing I am doing: I switch my attention to it and cease doing what I was doing before. The most common causes for such persistent thoughts are that there is something else that you could be doing which is more urgent than what you were working on at the time, that there is something left unfinished or wrong or dangerous in what you are doing, or that there is a nice ripe insight waiting to come into your awareness. If none of these things seem to

*Working meditation.*

be the case and there does not appear to be anything further to be learned from examining the thought, then switch your attention back to what you were doing before. If the thought still keeps coming up, allow yourself to stop again after a while and look at it another time, and so forth.

This ability to switch one's attention from one activity to another readily and without attachment does not come easily for most of us. With practice, it can be cultivated. In a training monastery the schedule is designed to help one learn this: when the bell sounds one stops what one is doing, bows, and goes to the next thing. You might think of certain aspects of your life as this bell: "intruding" but important thoughts, the boss's request to change everything you've just done, or the baby's crying. They are signals to "bow" and switch your attention to something else. I sometimes liken mindfulness training to driving on an icy road: keep a gentle, smooth control of the wheel, keep your eyes on the road—but don't ignore your peripheral vision, and when you see a truck skidding towards you, change course gently and don't insist on the right-of-way!

There are two common objections to the practice of every-minute meditation. The first is, "I'll never get my work done if I do only one thing at a time." This is a reasonable concern; fortunately it is usually unfounded. What actually happens for most people (after the initial few days of awkwardness when the whole thing can seem a bit strange and disruptive of one's habitual patterns of living) is that they can actually do more and better work by doing one thing at a time. I think what happens is that the time saved when one does several things at once is more than compensated for by the increased efficiency (and decreased tension) that results from devoting all of one's attention to the task at hand.

The second objection is that doing this is a lot of work and it interferes with customary social interactions. This is true, and it is for these reasons that I do not recommend doing it all the time, at least not for most people. Even in the monastic setting, a certain rest from this practice is built into the system, and the monks enjoy social conversation while drinking tea or eating an informal meal in the refectory. So, perhaps you may choose to eat breakfast and talk to your spouse at the same time, after all. Go ahead, and enjoy the meal together (but I'll bet you enjoy it more if you don't also try watching TV at the same time).

My advice, therefore, is to do one thing at a time (and pay attention to it) as much as it seems wise to do so, bring your mind back gently each time it wanders, but don't be so strict on yourself that you find the practice unpalatable. Done properly, the exercise of every-minute meditation is refreshing, liberating, and energizing. Together with formal seated meditation, it can make a significant contribution to increasing one's religious understanding. It is my favorite form of meditation.

* * *

# *Applying Meditation to Everyday Life.*

Rev. Jishō Perry, M.O.B.C.

The most common concept of education is that we learn from external stimuli—from books, lectures, art, music, TV, etc. There is another dimension to education; it comes from the literal meaning of the Latin which is to lead forth or draw out. This concept of education is to bring out that which is already there but not developed or fully understood. Socrates demonstrated the existence of past lives by showing that an uneducated slave boy already knew and understood profound mathematical truths by simply asking the boy questions and allowing him the opportunity of making the mental connections from the facts elicited. Although all of us have access to the Treasure House within us, we are not taught how to get at it. Putting meditation into practice is the process of learning how to be still within so that we can respond to the Buddha Nature within us. Out of the practice of serene reflection meditation arises the ability to be alert and sufficiently still in all activities so that we can fully use the capabilities we have. This does not make us gods or supermen; we still have the limitations of our humanity, but within those limitations there is another dimension which gradually opens up as the layers of ignorance are removed by spiritual training. Out of the ignorance we come to understanding: the alertness of meditation allows us to see the ignorance, the stillness allows us to plummet to its depths, and from there the understanding arises naturally when the selfish self is out of the way.

The underlying assumption here is that we are all part of the Cosmic Buddha and have the ability to be in contact with the Buddha Nature within us. This is the act of faith. When we act on faith we have the ability to be in touch with this adequacy or wholeness. To learn from anything, however, we must admit that there is something we do not know or do not understand. This creates an attitude of humility from which it is possible to accept knowledge and information. Both the willingness to admit that there is something we can learn and the acceptance of our own adequacy to learn it are essential. As Great Master Dōgen puts it:

> When we wish to teach and enlighten all things by ourselves, we are deluded; when all things teach and enlighten us, we are enlightened....[1]

We normally face the unknown with fear and inadequacy, which makes it very difficult to make the best choices or the most intelligent decisions. When this passes and we look through the eyes of humility from the knowledge of our own adequacy, which is no different from the willingness to grow and learn, then we can use the information—even the information of our own fears and inadequacies—effectively. This is when we actually learn something.

All this may seem somewhat irrelevant to the application of meditation to everyday life but, in fact, it is the very process of meditation, the sitting still within ourselves, that puts us in contact with both our own adequacy and our own humility. This opens the door to learn from everything. As we learn and grow we come to know that "the Light of Buddha is increasing in brilliance and the Wheel of the Dharma is always turning."[2]

Clarity arises naturally out of the effort of awareness. To pay attention is to stop putting our own ideas and opinions on the situation, simply and clearly to see things as they are. This is not a constant state. Clarity will arise and go as the sun arises and sets or goes behind a cloud only to reappear again. The more we make the effort, the more we see where that effort can be made. Each time we go through one door, the next one appears in the distance. Each time we see what there is to do, we also see how much we have not done. This need not be a source of discouragement or despair: it is doing the best we can when we see where we can do better and make the effort to do it. This is the "always going on, always becoming Buddha" of *The Scripture of Great Wisdom.*

Every day the kōan[3] arises and we have the opportunity to put meditation into practice. We need to push back the frustration line or not react to the anger button or not tense up the greed tentacle, if only just for a little longer than usual. If we can give a bit more energy to the situation before we act on the anger, wait just a little longer before giving in to the frustration or acting on the greed, then stillness deepens and often we find that the frustration, anger or greed disappears. Sometimes we act on the anger or the frustration; then the only way to put meditation into action is simply to accept the situation and the consequences that develop. There is no need to complicate the situation with judgments or with guilt.

The area of greatest difficulty in daily life is not necessarily mechanical tasks or competence in work or even the complications of our relationships with others, but it is the relationship we have with ourselves and our greater self, the Selfless Self or the Buddha Nature. It is often easier to see when greed, hate or opinions get in the way of others than it is to see it in ourselves and often harder to know what to do with it when we do see it. But whatever the external situation, the only thing that we really have to deal with is ourselves, and the basic rules for dealing with ourselves and others are set out simply in the Precepts.[4] External situations and what others do are not as important as how we respond to them. The Buddha rejects nothing and uses everything to teach and enlighten us. Beneath the surface tensions or distrust or ambition, greed or anger, guilt or fear, lies something deeper—a stillness that is undisturbed by the superficial waves. When we act from this place something within us responds and it also responds in those with whom we relate: Buddha recognizes Buddha. It still takes a great deal of effort, energy and compassionate awareness, i.e., meditation, to do this and to do it effectively. "Forget the selfish self for a little and allow the mind to remain natural for this is very close to the Mind that seeks the Way."[5]

Meditation must be done daily and in all facets of our lives. This meditation is the forgetting of the selfish self, not holding on to being hurt or angry, proud, friendly, compassionate, self-righteous, fearful, adequate or inadequate. Let all these things arise and let them go without clinging to or suppressing any of them. This is not an easy task because we have learned through many lifetimes to act on these manifestations of the self. If we want to truly go deeper and know the Cosmic Buddha for ourselves then we have no choice but to willingly give up our clinging to all selfish forms. These forms that currently bind us, however, are the source of our freedom. They are as a door which, while we cling to our suffering, remains closed; yet in our willingness to embrace and accept this selfish self, the door opens to genuine selflessness and a personal knowledge of something bigger and more wonderful than anything we can imagine or dream about. Buddhism does not require that we get rid of the selfish self, only that we do not indulge or suppress it. Out of that continual effort, the selfishness is converted into the Buddha Nature. Our realization of It will come and go and in the comings and the returnings our relationship to It will change, as will our relationships to all things both animate and inanimate.

When we chop onions we may have tears in our eyes and this may temporarily cloud our vision; we still have the responsibility to waste neither time nor the onion, nor chop our finger. Putting meditation into practice is just this. It requires being still within as we chop the onion. To get caught by the fear of possibly chopping our fingers or, through lack of awareness, to cut ourselves is to fall out of the stillness. Stop. Follow the breath up the spine as you inhale and down the sternum as you exhale and continue with the onion or go and bandage the finger. Do what needs to be done. Whether it is dealing with sickness or death, driving a car or simply wiping the dust from the table, it requires the same quality of meditation—awareness and a willingness to do better. We cannot clean the table effectively unless we can see where it is dirty; and so within ourselves we have to see where the dust of fears, greeds, angers, guilts, opinions, etc., have knocked us out of that fundamentally still place and know that this very dust contains all of the Buddha Nature and is not for one moment separate or apart from it.

Intellectual work also needs the application of meditation. To sift through the morass of information we have been fed and to allow what is relevant and useful to manifest itself naturally is to put meditation into practice. This same effort must also be used in working through misunderstandings and figuring out what it is that we and others have not understood. It is easy to get ourselves worked up over these misunderstandings or to ignore important points that need explanation. As meditation deepens, something nags at us not to ignore misunderstandings or to get bothered by them; just patiently persist when the opportunity arises. Learning to meditate will not make everything simple, easy, effortless, uncomplicated and efficient. Reality is bigger than that; life is more complex.

There is a persistent myth that meditation will make you a superman. On a spiritual level it will put you in touch with the certain knowledge that there is Something Indestructible, the Unborn and Undying, and that it is possible to be in contact with this limitless energy. However, It is not available for selfish use unless you want to create a hell for yourself. It is subject to the Laws of the Universe,[6] which include the Precepts. It is available through gratitude and respect. All this naturally unfolds through meditation and its application. However, no matter how far one goes in meditation, one still remains human; there are physical limitations, emotions, thoughts, feelings, times of difficulty and times of stress. One continually comes around again to the beginning, standing there naked and unashamed before the Lord of the House, and out of the ignorance and the willingness to "sit up straight in the presence of the Buddha,"[7] compassion, love and wisdom have already manifested themselves. To be completely human is itself the manifestation of the Buddha Nature. This is realized by putting meditation into practice. Out of that place of stillness, the Buddha Himself participates in both the suffering and the joy and is completely unmoved by either.

* * *

*Notes.*

1. Great Master Dōgen, "Genjo-kōan" ("The Problem of Everyday Life"), in *Zen is Eternal Life,* 3rd ed. rev., by Rōshi P.T.N.H. Jiyu-Kennett (Mt. Shasta, California: Shasta Abbey Press, 1987), p. 172.
2. See Rev. Master P.T.N.H. Jiyu-Kennett, M.O.B.C., *The Liturgy of the Order of Buddhist Contemplatives for the Laity* (Mt. Shasta, California: Shasta Abbey Press, 1987), p. 121.
3. Any spiritual problem or obstacle we think separates us from the Eternal.
4. For the Buddhist Precepts, see pp. 66–76.

5. Dōgen, "Gyakudo-yōjinshu" ("Important Aspects of Zazen"), in *Zen is Eternal Life,* by Jiyu-Kennett, p. 126.

6. The Five Laws of the Universe:

   The physical world is not answerable to my personal will.
   The Law of Change.
   The Law of Karma is inevitable and inexorable.
   Without fail evil is vanquished and good prevails; this too is inexorable.
   The intuitive knowledge of Buddha Nature occurs to all men.

7. Dōgen, "Shushōgi" ("Training and Enlightenment"), in *Zen is Eternal Life,* by Jiyu-Kennett, p. 157.

# *Kyojūkaimon and Commentary*

## *Giving and Receiving the Teaching of the Precepts.*

*Preceptor:–*

"The Great Precepts of the Buddhas are kept carefully by the Buddhas; Buddhas give them to Buddhas, Ancestors give them to Ancestors. The Transmission of the Precepts is beyond the three existences of past, present and future; enlightenment ranges from time eternal and IS even now. Shakyamuni Buddha, our Lord, Transmitted the Precepts to Makakashyo and he Transmitted them to Ananda; thus the Precepts have been Transmitted to me in the eighty-fifth generation. I am now going to give them to you, in order to show my gratitude for the compassion of the Buddhas, and thus make them the eyes of all sentient beings; this is the meaning of the Transmission of the Living Wisdom of the Buddhas. I am going to pray for the Buddha's guidance and you should make confession and be given the Precepts. Please recite this verse after me:–

*Preceptor followed by congregation:–*

> "All wrong actions, behaviour and karma, perpetrated by me from time immemorial, have been, and are, caused by greed, anger and delusion which have no beginning, born of my body, mouth and will; I now make full and open confession thereof.

*Preceptor alone:–*

Reprinted, with revisions, from Great Master Keizan and Rev. Jiyu-Kennett, Rōshi, *The Kyojūkaimon and Commentary* (Mt. Shasta, California: Shasta Abbey, 1977).

> "Now, by the guidance of the Buddhas and Ancestors, we can discard and purify all our karma of body, mouth and will and obtain great immaculacy; this is by the power of confession.

"You should now be converted to Buddha, Dharma and Sangha. In the Three Treasures there are three merits; the first is the true source of the Three Treasures;"—*there is an unborn, uncreated, unformed, undying, indestructible, the Lord of the House, That Which speaks in silence and in stillness, the "still, small voice."*

"The second merit is the presence in the past of Shakyamuni Buddha"—*all Those Who have truly transmitted Buddhism throughout eternity.*

"The Third is His presence at the present time,"—*all Those Who transmit the Truth, Who live by the Precepts and make them Their blood and bones, the Sangha, the embodiment of the Preceptual Truth of the Buddhas.*

"The highest Truth is called the Buddha Treasure,"—*the knowledge of That Which Is, the knowledge of the unformed, uncreated, unborn, undying, indestructible; the certainty, without doubt, of Its existence, the KNOWLEDGE of It within oneself, the Buddha LIVING within oneself, the Lord of the House Who directs all things. If you study true Buddhism you will become as the water wherein the Dragon dwells; it is necessary to know the true Dragon; it is necessary to ask the Dragon, the Lord of the House, at all times to help and to teach. Only if you give all that is required of the price that the Dragon asks will He show you the jewel; you must accept the jewel from the Dragon without doubting its value or querying the price.*

"Immaculacy is called the Dharma Treasure,"—*one must live with the roots of karma cut away. To do this we must indeed know the house-builder of this house of ego, know all his tools, know all his building materials; there is no other way that we can know immaculacy. The house-builder of the house of ego must be known absolutely, recognised at all times. It is not enough to have a kenshō; one must go back to the source of the karmic stream; one must return to that source to find out what set it going. Kenshō shows the slate is clean; to find the source of karma cuts its roots and, with constant training, keeps evil karma at a minimum but, since there is nothing from the first, there is nothing clean and nothing that is unclean—we cannot know this, however, until we have first tried to clean it. "Most houses can do with a thorough sweeping but even a million sweepings will not clear away the dust completely." Thus man remains in his body and accepts it, knowing that* NOTHING MATTERS, *that he is immaculate, always was and always will be. This is the immaculacy of the Dharma Treasure; this makes the immaculacy and harmony of the Sangha Treasure possible. It is the knowledge of the True Kesa, that which is immaculate above all dust and dirt, the knowledge that the dust and dirt are indeed a figment of one's own ego's imagination as a result of past, accrued karma, that makes possible the Transmission of the Light from the far past to the now and the far future without words. The Scriptures show up blank pages; there* IS *a Transmission that lies beyond them.*

"Harmony is the Sangha Treasure"—*this is brought about by the knowledge that, no matter what a member of the Sangha may do, he* IS *immaculate from the very beginning; there* IS *nothing from the first. "Thus shall ye think all this fleeting world, a star at dawn, a bubble in a stream, a child's laugh, a phantasm, a dream." Although this is true the members of the Sangha, the Zen Masters, all beings are bound by the law of karma; they will pay the price of what they do. Thus is the mind of the Sangha Treasure.*

"The Person Who has realised the Truth really is called the Buddha Treasure;"—*He* IS *the embodiment of the Truth, He* IS *Nirvana, He* IS *the Embodiment of Enlightenment, He* IS *the Treasure of the Buddha for, in Him, can be seen fully-digested, Preceptual Truth.*

"The Truth that is realised by Buddha is called the Dharma Treasure,"—*that is the* KNOWLEDGE *of the unborn, uncreated, unformed, undying, indestructible; the living with this knowledge without doubt, the trusting eternally of the Lord of the House, the certainty of the Treasure House within oneself at the gate of which sits the True Dragon Who* IS *indeed the Lord of the House.*

"The People who study that which lies within the Treasure House are called the Treasure of the Sangha,"—*the Dharma and the Sangha are one and the same thing, being the embodiment each of the other, if fully-digested, Preceptual Truth is their rule of life. If you ask, 'What is a monk?' you* KNOW *that it is his Kesa.*

"He Who teaches devas and humans is called the Buddha Treasure,"—*He Who gives true teaching, being beyond praise and blame, the holy and the unholy, right and wrong, without fear or favor, He Who becomes 'good' for others.*

"That which appears in the world in the Scriptures and is 'good' for others is called the Dharma Treasure,"—*anything may teach. However infinitesimally small, however large, no matter what, all things may teach the Dharma when they live by fully-digested, Preceptual Truth, when they have cut away the roots of karma, when they know the house-builder of the house of ego and are constantly keeping him from rebuilding again as a result of* PRACTISING *fully-digested, Preceptual Truth.*

"He who is released from all suffering and is beyond the world is called the Sangha Treasure;"—*he for whom no longer desires burn, wherein wants and cravings no longer exist; he who gets up in the morning and goes to sleep at night, eats when he is hungry, sleeps when he is tired, is satisfied with that which he is given and does not ask for more than he can absolutely use in the immediate now. When someone is converted to the Three Treasures thus, he can have the Precepts of the Buddhas absolutely.*

*In this manner you should make the True Buddha your teacher and not follow wrong ways. The True Buddha that is your Teacher is indeed the Lord of the House, the True Dragon. Do not hold on to your tiny kenshō; trust the Lord of the House, hold fast by Him no matter what state you may be in, whether you are well or sick, brightly alive or dying, hold fast by the Lord of the House.*

## *The Three Pure Precepts*

"CEASE FROM EVIL.

This is the house of all the laws of Buddha; this is the source of all the laws of Buddha." *The law of karma is one of the five laws of the universe; it is absolute, it is inescapable. All are bound by the law of karma once it is set in motion. By accident someone made the course of karma; it is not intentionally set in motion; what happens, or happened, or will happen to you or to anyone else is caused by karma; by accident the wheel rolled the wrong way. Do not continue the rolling of the wheel in the wrong direction by dwelling on the past or fearing the future; live now without evil. Stop the wheel* NOW *by cutting the roots of karma, by knowing the house-builder of the house of ego; if you do not, karma will go on endlessly. The only difference between you and another being is that* YOU *have the opportunity of knowing the Lord of the House right now, having heard the teachings of the Buddha. Others may have less opportunity than you but, when they hear it, who knows which will be first at the gate of the Treasure House? "Cease from evil" is absolute, in thought, in word, in deed, in body, in spirit. All are bound by the law of karma; do not doubt this. You will pay for everything you do if you do not cut the roots* NOW *and live by fully-digested, Preceptual Truth. Do not worry about the karma of others; each man his karma makes.*

"DO ONLY GOOD.

The Dharma of Shakyamuni Buddha's Enlightenment is the Dharma of all existence." *Do not do anything unless it is 'good;' do not do anything unless you have first asked the Lord of the House if it is good for you to do it. Do nothing whatsoever in a hurry; do nothing whatsoever on the spur of the moment unless you know the CERTAINTY given by the Lord of the House; know that you must take the consequences of what you do if it is not a fully-digested act for YOU know What lies beyond good and evil, right and wrong; YOU know That Which lies beyond morality; you KNOW the Lord of the House. Ask the Lord of the House at all times before you do anything whatsoever. "Is it good? Is it Your will?" If you do not ask the Lord of the House, the house-builder of the house of ego will again pick up his tools and, before you know it, there will be a great structure from which you must again escape. If a thing is 'good' in this way it may be done; if it is not 'good' in this way it should not be done; I am not speaking here of good and evil; I am speaking of 'good' in the sense of IF IT IS RIGHT; this is beyond right and wrong; IF IT IS GOOD is beyond good and evil. This teaching is indeed the teaching of Shakyamuni Buddha's enlightenment for there was not one of His acts that was not the result of fully-digested, Preceptual Truth. If you live thus, doing that only which is 'good' after you have asked the Lord of the House, after you KNOW the TRUE Lord of the House, then you can KNOW the teaching of Shakyamuni Buddha's enlightenment and know that His enlightenment and yours are identically the same; but this is only if you know Who the Lord of the House is and do not suffer from the idea that YOU are the Lord of the House. Always you must ask the Lord of the House; always you must be humble in His presence. "Please teach me that which it is good for me to do this day. Please show me that which it is good for me to teach this day. Please give me the certainty that I teach the Truth and know, indeed, that, when the still, small voice within my mind and heart says 'Yes' I must obey that teaching. When it says 'No' I must NOT disobey that teaching." When the Lord speaks spring up joyfully to answer; then, indeed, it is good to do anything whatsoever He asks; KNOW that the Lord will NEVER break the Precepts.*

"DO GOOD FOR OTHERS.

Be beyond both the holy and the unholy. Let us rescue ourselves and others." *Do not set up a chain of causation that will cause others to do wrong; do not do that which will cause another to grieve; do not do that which will result in your creating karma for another being; do not accidentally set the wheel of karma in motion. Do not let yourself hear the words, "What demon allowed you to become a priest? From what demon did you learn Buddhism?" To be beyond both the holy and the unholy, to be beyond praise and blame, to act only from what the Lord of the House teaches without worrying whatsoever what the world may think is indeed to have understood the Three Pure Precepts. Before any act is performed you must ask yourself, "Am I ceasing from evil in doing this act? Is it good in the sight of the Lord of the House? Shall I cause another being to do harm either to himself or to others? I cannot stop HIM doing harm, for each man his karma makes and must carry for himself, but I can do that about myself which will prevent ME from accidentally starting the course of karma. I must think carefully of my every act. I may not cause another to make a mistake in Buddhism." By so doing we rescue both ourselves and others for, in cutting the roots of karma for ourselves, we cut the roots of karma for others also.* "These three are called the Three Pure Precepts." *Without them one cannot live the Buddhist life.*

## *The Ten Great Precepts*

"DO NOT KILL.

No life can be cut off for the Life of Buddha is increasing. Continue the Life of Buddha and do not kill Buddha." *Above all, do not turn your face away from Buddha, the Lord of the House, for this is indeed to commit spiritual suicide; to kill Buddha is to turn away from Buddha. "Man stands in his own shadow and wonders why it is dark and only he can turn round." To turn away from Buddha is to say, "My ego is greater than the Lord of the House; my opinions are more right; my wishes are more important." It is* YOU *whom you kill. If you do not listen to the Lord of the House in this life, in what life will you listen to the Lord of the House? Will you for eternity attempt to commit* REAL *suicide? If you always face the Buddha you will always know Buddha; if you always listen to the Lord of the House there is no possibility of your ever killing anything.*

"DO NOT STEAL.

The mind and its object are one. The gateway to enlightenment stands open wide." *There is nothing whatsoever that can be stolen. "Preserve well for you now have," says the Scripture; each of us possesses the Treasure House. All we have to do is ask the Dragon for permission to enter, ask the Dragon if we may see the jewel and it will be given to us. He who tries to rob himself, he who tries to steal from the Treasure House can never have the Treasure; erudition is as this; taking drugs is as this. All you have to do is ask the Lord of the House and you may know and possess all things. The gateway to enlightenment does indeed stand open wide for the true mind of the Buddha and the jewel are one and the same; ask the Lord of the House at all times and the gates will be thrown wide open. Remember that he "who counts another's treasure can never have his own;" he who steals can only ever rob himself.*

"DO NOT COVET.

The doer, the doing and that which has the doing done to it are immaculate therefore there is no desire. It is the same doing as that of the Buddhas." *Thus there is nothing to be coveted and not one that covets. "Preserve well for you now* HAVE,*" says the Scripture. Since there is nothing from the first, how can there be anything to preserve well? "The white snow falls upon the silver plate; the snowy heron in the bright moon hides; resembles each the other yet these two are not the same." Thus we think there is a difference; thus we think there is an ability to covet and something* TO *covet; thus man makes mistakes. Indeed there* IS *nothing from the first.*

"DO *NOT SAY THAT WHICH IS NOT TRUE.*

The Wheel of the Dharma rolls constantly and lacks for nothing yet needs something." *The Dharma is Truth Itself but it needs expression. He who lies does not allow the Dharma to show itself, he does not allow the Dharma to be expressed, he does not allow the world to see the Dharma Wheel in action. And still* "the sweet dew covers the whole world," *including those who lie,* "and within that dew lies the Truth."

"DO *NOT SELL THE WINE OF DELUSION.*

There is nothing to be deluded about. If we realise this we are enlightenment itself." *"Thus shall ye think of all this fleeting world, a star at dawn, a bubble in a stream, a child's laugh, a phantasm, a dream." If you hold on to nothing whatsoever there can be no delusion nor can there be enlightenment; then there are no opposites. Thus, indeed, we are enlightenment itself—yet always we will have the form and figure of old monks.*

"DO *NOT SPEAK AGAINST OTHERS."*

*Do not speak against the Lord of the House. Every person, every being* IS *the Temple of the Lord wherein the Lord dwells, the still water wherein the Dragon lives. If you speak against others you speak against the Lord of the House. Do not try to divide the Lord of the House; do not try to cause war within the Lord; do not try to make the Lord make war upon Himself.* "In Buddhism, the truth and everything are the same;

the same law, the same enlightenment and the same behaviour. Do not allow any one to speak of another's faults." *Do not find fault with the Lord of the House.* "Do not allow any one to make a mistake in Buddhism." *To speak against the Lord of the House is the gravest mistake of which I know.*

"DO NOT BE PROUD OF YOURSELF AND DEVALUE OTHERS."

*It is enough for me to* KNOW *the Lord of the House, to know that He dwells within all things. How can there be devaluation of others if they are the Temple of the Lord? How can there be pride if all possess equally within the Lord?* "Every Buddha and every Ancestor realises that He is the same as the limitless sky and as great as the universe. When They realise Their true body there is nothing within or without; when They realise Their true body They are nowhere more upon the earth." *There is nothing to be proud of and nothing to be devalued.*

"DO NOT BE MEAN IN GIVING EITHER DHARMA OR WEALTH."

*Since all possess the Lord, there is nothing to be given and nothing to be taken away, and still all things must be given, all things offered at all times and in all places.* "One phrase, one verse, the hundred grasses,"—*all contain the Lord, all express the Lord—each in its own way and each perfectly.* "One Dharma, one enlightenment, every Buddha, every Ancestor." *No difference, nothing greater, nothing smaller; nothing truer, nothing less true. When all is within the Lord, all stand straight together, a million Buddhas stand in one straight line. Out of gratitude to the Buddhas and Ancestors we give Dharma, we give wealth, we give life itself—strength, youth, beauty, wealth, everything that we have and, even then, we cannot give thanks enough for one second of their true training; we can never repay their kindness to us. Only by our own true training is the possible and then, again, there is no repayment; it is just the work of a Buddha.*

"Do not be angry.

There is no retiring, no going, no Truth, no lie; there is a brilliant sea of clouds, there is a dignified sea of clouds." *Just there is that going on which causes us to see unclearly; but if we truly look, if we look with care, we will see that the true and beautiful sky is shining behind the clouds; we may see the Lord of the House. No matter how angry the person is who is with us, we may see in him, too, the Lord if we are truly looking, if our own ego is out of the way and, in seeing the Lord in him, he can see the Lord in us. The depth of the ocean is still even when there is a great storm upon its surface; thus should we be when there is anger, knowing that nothing whatsoever can touch the Truth.*

"Do not defame the Three Treasures.

To do something by ourselves, without copying others, is to become an example to the world and the merit of doing such a thing becomes the source of all wisdom. Do not criticise but accept everything." *The Lord of the House does not do things in the normally accepted ways, nor do the Buddhas and Ancestors; They are not individual and They are not the same as each other. Each expresses the Truth in His own way as do all things; They do that which is Their way and express the Lord within it. Do not criticise the way of another, do not call it into question; look within it and see the Lord. Look with the mind of a Buddha and you will see the heart of a Buddha. To criticise is to defame the Lord of the House. Love the Lord of the House at all times—know Him, talk to Him; never let a day go by when you do not consult with Him even on the slightest matter. Then you will never, as long as you live, defame the Three Treasures.*

"These sixteen Precepts are thus.
Be obedient to the teaching and its giving; accept it with bows."

# *Reading The Kyojūkaimon and Commentary.*

David Powers, Lay Minister, O.B.C.

One of the most useful and powerful parts of my training is the daily reading of *The Kyojūkaimon and Commentary,* the sixteen Precepts, together with the commentary of Great Master Keizan and of Rev. Master Jiyu-Kennett. When I first began reading *The Kyojūkaimon and Commentary,* I must say I had only a very foggy idea of what it was about. But as I continued to read it and meditate, things began to become more clear. Sometimes one of the Precepts has seemed to come to life and stand out in relief as I went about my daily business. The two particular Precepts with which this has happened are:

*"Do not speak against others."*

*Do not speak against the Lord of the House. Every person, every being is the Temple of the Lord wherein the Lord dwells, the still water wherein the Dragon lives. If you speak against others you speak against the Lord of the House. Do not try to divide the Lord of the House; do not try to cause war within the Lord; do not try to make the Lord make war upon Himself.* "In Buddhism, the Truth and everything are the same; the same law, the same enlightenment and the same behaviour. Do not allow any one to speak of another's faults." *Do not find fault with the Lord of the House.* "Do not allow any one to make a mistake in Buddhism." *To speak against the Lord of the House is the gravest mistake of which I know.*

This article first appeared in the *Berkeley Buddhist Priory Newsletter*, Fall, 1981.

> *"Do not be proud of yourself and devalue others."*
>
> *It is enough for me to KNOW the Lord of the House, to know that He dwells within all things. How can there be devaluation of others if they are the Temple of the Lord? How can there be pride if all possess equally within the Lord?* "Every Buddha and every Ancestor realises that He is the same as the limitless sky and as great as the universe. When They realise Their true body there is nothing within or without; when They realise Their true body They are nowhere more upon the earth." *There is nothing to be proud of and nothing to be devalued.*[1]

One day I began to realize that I was breaking these Precepts time after time during the day, so I started to make an effort to keep them. The first thing that happened was that I found I had about twenty-five to fifty percent less to say during my normal conversations when I quit judging, criticizing or making fun of others. Although dramatic, this change was not too difficult, once I made the effort. However, the next level in keeping the first of these Precepts was much more subtle and difficult. I would find myself listening to others criticize someone else and to some extent supporting them just by nodding my head slightly or rolling my eyes or with a facial expression that indicated consent. These little gestures of consent would frequently result in two or three minutes of breaking the Precepts with criticism. When I began to stop doing this the effect it had on my interactions was surprising, and after a while people tended not to run someone or something down when I was around.

Reading *The Kyojūkaimon and Commentary* has also had other effects. For example, there have been times when I was just about to do something (or in the middle of it) when one of the Precepts would come to mind, like, "Cease from evil." At these times the Precepts have kept me out of a fair amount of trouble. At other times I have been pondering over a decision (like, should I write off this lunch as a business expense or was it social?), when I just stop and turn to the Precepts. There is "Do not steal," and the decision is suddenly easier. I do not have to think, "Will I be audited by the IRS, and if so can I prove that we talked about business?" The truth is it was just a friendly lunch, not business, and the decision is that simple.

It is important when putting the Precepts into practice to use them as a guide to avoid mistakes and not to use them to be unnecessarily harsh with oneself. For example, in the above case it is useful to recognize that declaring a lunch as a business expense, when it is not, would be making a mistake. However there is no benefit in going beyond this and saying that I am training poorly because I almost broke the Precepts and therefore I am *bad*. It can be a very severe mistake to misuse the Precepts in this way, and in fact one is actually breaking the Precepts by so doing. I have found the Precepts to be most helpful when used as a gentle guide to point the way when faced with the decisions and problems of everyday life. It is not possible to keep all of the Precepts literally at all times, but we must do the very best we can.

One of the things that surprised me about trying to keep the Precepts was that some of them actually get a little easier with practice. A good example is anger. When I started out trying not to get angry it seemed almost impossible. This was because when I realized that I was angry, the anger was already overwhelming. It was like trying to stop Niagara Falls. But with some persistence, I began to notice my anger as it started to arise. When I was able to see the anger arising, it also became easier not to get caught up in it. The anger did not disappear, but I did not necessarily have to do anything with it, such as yell at someone or defend myself. Sometimes the anger just comes and goes very quickly when I recognize it and do not get tangled up in it and feed energy into it. This is like a large boulder sitting at the top of a hill. Once the boulder starts to roll down the hill it gathers momentum and becomes more and more difficult to stop. But if you watch the boulder very carefully at the top of the hill and see when it just begins to teeter, you can steady it without too much effort. Trying to keep the Precepts is like carefully watching the boulder. The more you practice, the better you get at keeping the boulder balanced and seeing when it starts to teeter. In this way one of the big problems that comes up for me is now much easier to train with than it was when I first started.

The thing that is most helpful to me about reading and taking the Precepts is that I can do it *now*. I do not have to wait until I have more faith, or until I decide if I want to be a monk, or until I go to a meditation retreat or until everything is *just right*. The Precepts are something that I can put into my everyday training now and they get straight to the heart of what I am trying to do. Reading *The Kyojūkaimon and Commentary* takes me about twenty to thirty minutes. It is important to read in a place where there is as little distraction as possible and to give yourself fully to reading without the diversion of a cup of coffee or conversation. Reading just before meditation, or just after, also seems to be helpful. I try to read *The Kyojūkaimon and Commentary* every day, or half one day and half the next if there is not time all at once. I am sure that it would also be helpful to read it twice a week or once a week if that is all the time one can find. The benefit seems to come from reading and practicing on a regular basis so that the Precepts weave themselves into the fabric of our everyday life in the same way that daily meditation does.

* * *

*Note.*

1. Pp. 74–75 of this publication.

# *The Practice of Wisdom.*

Rev. Kinzan Learman, M.O.B.C.

When I was first introduced to Buddhist training, three things were said to be very important: the first was to keep the Precepts, the second was meditation and the third was wisdom. At the time, I was very keen to learn meditation and so concentrated my effort on keeping up my meditation practice and trying to operate on the principle of doing good for all things, both animate and inanimate, for both myself and others. As my training deepened, I came more and more to see the great value of keeping the Precepts *in detail;* I also came to see that the practice of meditation and keeping the Precepts go hand in hand. And later still, I came to see that these two are both the means to and the expression of wisdom.

Because the real keeping of the Precepts embodies the harmonization of body and mind, the harmonization of self with others—the harmonization of oneself with the Way of the Buddhas and Ancestors—unless one is willing to keep the Precepts, one is not going to want to practice serene reflection meditation. It will become too painful. This is because the consequences of what we do become much clearer to us through this kind of meditation than might otherwise be the case, even though the consequences of our actions are always reflected within our own minds and bodies whether we choose to recognize them or not. For instance, people who take huge risks often worry and develop stomach ulcers. Alcoholism is frequently the result

Reprinted, with changes, from *The Journal of Shasta Abbey,* vol. XIII, nos. 11 and 12: 37–43.

of an unwillingness to face oneself completely, and all other tensions and pains are due to past unwholesome or misguided karma. As *The Most Excellent Mirror—Samādhi* says: "If you should go against the basic Truth, you come to a dead end."[1] Many such relationships between what we think, say and do, and how we feel, become apparent when we pay attention in the right way, yet attachment to ultimately destructive habits may run deep. We do not always *want* to recognize attitudes and behavior for what they are, because we are scared of what change may mean to us. To meditate, however, is to be open to seeing clearly the results of our actions. The first warning that we may be heading for a showdown with deep-seated attachments is when we find excuses for not meditating. Unless we notice this tendency and resolve to continue our practice, we gradually lose interest and eventually stop. Another way it may manifest is when we find ourselves at a tolerable plateau or even at an impasse. The same old difficulty keeps nagging at us in different ways, but we never seem to be able to deal with it properly. Patience, persistence and a willingness to embrace the difficulty and go deeper through a keener awareness of what has or is happening are in order. And a willingness to change whatever attitude or behavior that may be necessary in order to resolve the difficulty is absolutely essential.

Great Master Dōgen says in the "Genjo-kōan" ("The Problem of Everyday Life"):

> to observe objects and voices, with complete awareness of body and mind, is very different from seeing a reflection in a mirror or the moon reflected in water; even if you see one side of something the other will still be in shadow.[2]

The "moon reflected in water" is an analogy for the enlightenment that a person can reach. Dōgen in this instance, however, is saying: do not look for pie-in-the-sky 'enlightenment'; do everything with complete awareness of your own body and mind, *look inwards* and you will know if your actions create harmony or suffering. And you will come to know not just when you have made mistakes—which result in pain and turmoil—but also when you do something right. You will feel it: your heart will be warmed, your mind will be set at ease, there will be a deep-seated sense that what you are doing is *right*.

On the surface, it may appear that Buddhist training is self-centered. But such training is *not* to block out the world. This is one reason why we meditate with our eyes open. We are, however, trying to become aware of our inner life as well as our outer circumstances, because what goes on within us and what goes on around us are inextricably related. There *is* Something that lies within and yet beyond the world. It is unsubstantial, yet knowable and real. So, the object of contemplation is not 'self', nor selfish. We do not push away the myriad phenomena commonly known as our 'selves'—the thoughts, sensations, emotions, habits and viewpoints—that arise, lest we become hard, callous and lacking in compassion. If we get caught up in them, however, the possibility of acting wisely is lost. The point of meditation is to allow That which is real Compassion to work within and through us. The Four Wisdoms of charity, tenderness, benevolence and sympathy[3] arise out of this effort.

Just as meditation is basic to Buddhist practice and gives rise to a real and vital desire to keep the Precepts, so too do our wholehearted efforts to keep the Precepts form the basis of all Buddhist activity and give rise to the necessity of meditation.

At one point, I came across the teaching that the Discipline (keeping the Precepts) is the work of a monk.

This perplexed me at the time for all the monks had responsibilities, which I considered to be our 'work'. Cooking, cleaning, building, fixing, writing letters, taking care of guests, tending the sick and the animals, doing ceremonies and giving retreats—were not these our work? Upon reflection, however, it became clear that each of these activities and, indeed, all *real* work comes out of our effort to keep the Precepts. We grow and prepare food lest we become lean and die; we maintain the fabric of the monastery lest it becomes unsanitary and unsafe and thereby a hazard to ourselves and others; we offer the merit of our ceremonies and give retreats lest we become mean with the wealth of the Dharma. Likewise, all that is done in the monastery has its basis in keeping the Precepts. It did occur to me, however, that it is extremely valuable to consider the *Precepts* to be the work and allow everything else to evolve out of them. It is very easy to become so attached to, caught up in or confused by our livelihoods that we lose sight of our real purpose and allow ourselves to do harm instead: a contractor who builds homes (shelter being one of the four necessities of life) on a toxic waste dump because he needs the money would be an example of this. It is extremely important to realize that what really matters is to keep the Precepts and to have the courage to follow them through. On the surface, there may not be, and usually there will not be, a clearcut or easy solution to many of the problems of life. When we are placed in such a position, the necessity of meditation becomes extremely clear, for it is within the attitude of all-acceptance and nonattachment, which is the essence of serene reflection meditation, that we allow the Way to manifest.

Indeed, meditation and keeping the Precepts do go hand in hand. I would like to tell a story that shows the results of getting caught up in one's *head* about keeping the Precepts.

One Friday afternoon the monastery was getting ready for a big community work project that was to take place on the weekend. We had extra people lined up and a deadline to meet. About 4:30 p.m., however, our truck broke down. It was a key element of the project, so we were under a great deal of pressure to get it repaired. As our usual garage was booked up and being in charge of our Maintenance Department, I was responsible for coming up with the best solution possible under the circumstances. Now something inside me said, "Take it to Yreka," and when I checked with the garage there, they said they could get to it during the next work week. Although another local garage offered to start the work on Saturday morning, I continued to get the message that we should "Take it to Yreka."

Now our Treasurer was not keen for this plan. Because of the extra time and expense, he wanted to try the local garage. Although I expressed my preference for Yreka, my first mistake was not to have sufficient faith in my meditation: I did not impress upon him the clarity of my feeling and went along with his suggestion instead. Upon arriving at the garage office, everything in me said, "Get *out* of here!" My reaction was the thought, "I can't do that! What would they and the Treasurer think of me!"—fear of breaking the appointment for no tangible reason other than a gut feeling that something was really wrong was my second mistake. My third mistake was to act on that fear: I justified leaving the truck with them with the thought that, "All beings have Buddha Nature. I ought to be able to trust them."

Three months later and three clutches later, we had to take the garage to court because it was unable to fix a routine clutch problem and refused to refund our money. We finally did take the truck to Yreka and had no problem getting it repaired and back on the road. For me, however, there were a number of valuable lessons. The first one was that through meditation one *can* know what is the right course of action, and we have a responsibility to pay attention to it. Second, because all beings have Buddha Nature, it does not necessarily follow that you can trust your truck with them! And third, the Precepts are useless when they are applied from the head and not from meditation.

Now there are many levels at which to keep the Precepts; they point to much more than such gross mistakes as killing, bald dishonesty and deliberate carelessness, etc. For instance, there can be errors of omission as well as commission. A teacher who expects too little from her students wastes their full potential. This is a form of stealing. Furthermore, right actions for wrong reasons can have very hollow results. To take a job primarily for the social status that goes along with it and not for the joy of doing the work is an example. In studying Great Master Keizan's commentary on the Precepts in the *Kyojūkaimon,*[4] one comes to see that he is pointing to the basic enlightened standpoint that allows us to keep the Precepts. We need not covet because, from the standpoint of enlightenment, there is nothing to be desired. All that we truly need is, and always will be, offered. We need not feel compelled to kill because the real 'me' cannot be threatened. The Precepts arise naturally out of our training to point us back to enlightenment, back to 'no-self'. They are as a warning for us not to step off into duality, and the practice of Preceptual Truth requires the subtlety, the selflessness, of serene reflection meditation.

From the above, I hope that it is clear that real wisdom is *practiced.* True insight into the nature of the universe has a direct bearing on how one lives: the Precepts are the life of someone who is one with Great Wisdom.

There is a very wonderful story that Great Master Dōgen relates at the end of the "Genjo-kōan." In the following, if you understand for the word *wind, Buddha Nature, the Unborn;* for the word *stationary, unchanging;* and for the words *fan* and *fanning, training,* the meaning of the story becomes clear.

> One summer day a Zen teacher sat fanning himself when a monk asked, "Since the nature of wind is stationary and universally present, why do you use a fan?" The teacher replied, "Although you know its nature to be stationary, you do not know why it is universally present." "Why is it universally present?" asked the monk: for answer the teacher merely continued fanning himself and the monk bowed: the True Way of Transmission and enlightenment, which is the result of real experience, is the same as this. One who thinks that fanning is not needed, simply because wind is stationary by nature and requires no fan since it can be sensed, understands nothing whatsoever of its nature and its eternal presence: it is because it is eternally here that the wind of Buddhism makes the earth golden and the rivers run with ghee.[5]

* * *

*Notes.*

1. See Rev. Master P.T.N.H. Jiyu-Kennett, M.O.B.C., *The Liturgy of the Order of Buddhist Contemplatives for the Laity* (Mt. Shasta, California: Shasta Abbey Press, 1987), p. 64.
2. See *Zen is Eternal Life* by Rōshi P.T.N.H. Jiyu-Kennett, 3rd ed. rev. (Mt. Shasta, California: Shasta Abbey Press, 1987), p. 172.
3. See Great Master Dōgen, "Shushōgi" ("What is Truly Meant by Training and Enlightenment"), ibid., p. 160.
4. See pp. 66–76 of this publication.
5. See Great Master Dōgen, "Genjo-kōan" ("The Problem of Everyday Life"), in Jiyu-Kennett, *Zen is Eternal Life*, p. 176.

# *The Ten Precepts Meeting:*

## *The Ceremony of Daily Life.*

Rev. Ekō Little, M.O.B.C.

*[Held annually, the week-long Ten Precepts Meeting retreat is designed for those trainees who wish to take refuge in the Three Treasures and commit themselves to keeping the rest of the Precepts as well, thereby becoming lay Buddhists.]*

Welcome to those of you who are here for the first time; it is very nice to see you. To those who are coming back to be here again, it is wonderful to see you. I love to see people come at this time of year because I have never forgotten my first Ten Precepts Meeting. I hope that, if this is your first, you will look back on it as one of the more joyous occasions in your life; hopefully, one of *the* most joyous.

Because some of you are doing this for the first time, I want to explain the ceremonies in a little bit of detail and because some of you have done this many times before, I would also like to talk about what the Ten Precepts Meeting means, about the aspects of training that arise as a result of doing these ceremonies.

What does it mean to take part in the Ten Precepts Meeting? What does it mean to be a Buddhist? To me, implicit in being a Buddhist is the idea of searching for something: one's life has been found to be incomplete somehow and no matter what one does, no matter what sort of job one has or friends one has, there is this feeling that something is still missing. Perhaps, if you have had a certain amount of experience in Buddhist training, you can say that what you search for is the Lord of the House or the Cosmic Buddha. I remember that when I came to Buddhism,

This is an edited transcript of an informal talk given by Rev. Ekō Little at the beginning of the Ten Precepts retreat held at Shasta Abbey in 1983. It is reprinted, with changes, from *The Journal of Shasta Abbey*, vol. XIV, no. 2: 2–14.

however, it was not that clear to me, and for many of us it may be difficult to say that we know what it is we are searching for because what we are looking for is beyond the bounds of our ordinary mind or ordinary level of consciousness. So there is nothing wrong with your being here and not knowing what it is that you are looking for. The most important thing is that you are looking and that you want to find it.

Because nothing in the world has been able to satisfy the longing of our hearts, we begin to look inside ourselves. This is the beginning of the Buddha seeking for the Buddha; it is what brings us to the Ten Precepts Meeting and what eventually leads us to the night of recognition. It is the Buddha seeking for Itself, the Buddha longing for Itself and, eventually, finding Itself, which is what we call the realization of one's Buddha Nature. Everyone has Buddha Nature; everyone possesses It. But to really bring It forth, to make It shine and to make It a reality, one has to train. One has to use one's willingness to cultivate this desire and this longing in order that it may change from a little belief or a doubt that makes you question what you are doing to a reality that fills your whole life. The more you train, the more it happens.

The ceremonies for the Opening of the Gate of the Ten Precepts show you what you can do in your Buddhist training every day of your life. It is said that in religious training there are cooler and warmer moments. There are times when things are really happening, when it is extremely rough and all you can do is hold on. These times may be a bit easier to deal with than the times when nothing seems to be happening and everything is arid or empty: every day you seem to be just going along and nothing is happening, nothing is moving. These ceremonies show you how to deepen your training no matter what state of mind and body you happen to be in. The week of the Ten Precepts Meeting is somewhat dramatic, but what you should be able to find during it and what you should be able to carry back with you into your daily life is an understanding that the Ten Precepts Meeting can be every day for you. The ceremonies will not be of great use unless you can find something that you can apply to your everyday life, to your everyday training.

It is interesting to note that, with the exception of the Ceremony of Following Where the Precepts, as the Blood of the Buddhas, Lead, almost all the ceremonies take place at night. Whether this is by accident or design (probably a little bit of both), it is interesting to note that they take place in darkness. Darkness should be home to a Buddhist trainee because, to some degree or another, one's life is filled with darkness. There is nothing wrong with that, as we shall see; but in each of these ceremonies, you will find that you move from darkness into light and go back out into darkness again.

The first ceremony that we will be doing is the Ceremony of the Reading of the Ten Precepts. The Japanese word for this, *Kyojūkaimon,* is translated as "giving and receiving the teaching of the Precepts." It is interesting that the Japanese characters not only mean accepting the Precepts, but also giving them for, when we practice the Precepts we also give them to others. I shall explain this more fully later on.

You can make a commitment to keep the Precepts for a day, for a week, for a month, for a year—for your whole life. In practice, however, you can only ever take them for now. Their meaning will change and will grow as your training deepens and at each moment you will have to *want* to take them. The next time you are in the ceremony hall and you have a few moments, go into the Āchalanātha shrine which is on the left-hand side of the main altar. Āchalanātha is one of the Kings of Light and he stands in the middle of flames of fire holding a lariat and a sword. He uses the lariat to grab demons and tie them up, and he uses the sword to cut through delusion. I often think of the rope as the Precepts with which, in the beginning, we bind ourselves up. We tie ourselves up with them and we do so willingly. With the sword, we cut through delusion. A good word for delusion is also confusion. Therefore, Āchalanātha stands in the middle of fire holding the sword and the lariat as if to say, "If you wish to take the Precepts, if you wish to tie yourself up with them, if you wish to accept the difficulty of trying to follow them in daily life, here they are for you!"

The Precepts start with natural morality: we all know the consequences of killing, stealing, lying, etc. But as our training deepens, the Precepts begin to take on a deeper significance. I have heard Rev. Master Jiyu-Kennett explain that the Precepts help you to see the *whole* of the Cosmic Buddha. That is their purpose. They are not there to get in your way; they are there to help you. They are like the guard-rails on the freeway: there are six lanes to move in but you don't go past the guardrail over here, and you don't go past the guardrail over there, and all along the way, they help you get to where you are going. In the *kaimon* of *Kyojūkaimon,* the character for *kai* means "precept" and *mon* means "gate." Truly, accepting the Precepts is the gateway into the Buddhist Way.

Āchalanātha stands in the midst of flames, i.e., Āchalanātha stands in the midst of hell. It is good to know that hell in a Judeo-Christian context means something a little different from the hell the Buddhist is talking about. The Buddhist term for hell in this context is *samsara,* the constantly turning wheel of birth and death. Āchalanātha stands amid the flames of suffering, which are part of physical existence. He is also called the Great Immobile One and this explains the ferocity of his image. He is the Bodhisattva of awareness, steadfastness and immobility. He is just going to sit there; he is going to take the Precepts; he is going to cut through confusion and there are no two ways about it. So Āchalanātha is a very good expression of what arises naturally when you meditate. Everyone likes Avalokiteshwara because Avalokiteshwara looks like such a gentle lady, but it is important to look at some of the other

Bodhisattvas too and see what they are trying to teach. You *do* have to be a bit fierce, in a positive sense, in order to train properly; you have to have courage. Courage is another word for will; and the only thing that stops the will is fear—"the only thing to fear is fear itself." Once you become really familiar with the home of your own meditation, once you know That to which the Precepts are pointing, fear is never going to stop you again.

The most important thing in taking the Precepts is to understand the idea of intention because taking the Precepts and training yourself does not mean that you stop making mistakes. That you sometimes break them is sad, but the important thing is that your intention is to always keep them, to the best of your ability. The whole key to taking the Precepts is that you *want* to keep them; and when you find that you have made a mistake, you don't have to hide and say, "Oh my gosh, I've broken the Precepts, what am I going to do?" You "sit up straight in the presence of the Buddhas" and say, "Yes, I now realize that I made this mistake and I am not going to do it again." Then you go right on from there. When understood properly, the taking of the Precepts does not add another veneer of the fear and guilt that so many of us grow up with; but, instead, they are a tool that will free you from them. The Precepts embody a morality (I use that word with some trepidation because of the connotations it has in our culture) that actually sets you free.

What sometimes happens when people take the Precepts is that they go on and train for some time until they begin to notice that something within themselves, despite the fact that they *want* to keep the Precepts, keeps coming up and getting in the way. We all have our own particular recipe for suffering, whether it is in the form of fear or anger or lust or confusion: the details of suffering are different for every person, yet its root is the same for all of us. Often it can get to the point where you feel like there is almost another person inside of you saying, "I don't want to do that!" or "I've *got* to do that!" Should a person be unforewarned, it can lead him to doubt himself: he thinks he must be doing something wrong in training. It is important to realize, however, that the arising of this seeming obstruction does not damage or diminish the sincerity of your intention; it does show you that you need to train yourself more. As time goes on, the more you commit yourself to training and take refuge in the Three Treasures, the more this little fellow that we call "self" actually becomes your best friend because it is the very vehicle that leads you to the Truth. Another word for the arising of self is the *kōan* and it is quite normal for it to "arise naturally in daily life," as Great Master Dōgen says in *Rules for Meditation*. The kōan is not only the vehicle for suffering, but also for enlightenment. If you study it and take refuge in the teachings, it will lead you into a deeper understanding of the Precepts and enlightenment.

The next ceremony, after the Ceremony of the Reading of the Ten Precepts, is the Ceremony of Lay Ordination. Within our school of Buddhism, a trainee is *ordained* as a lay Buddhist only once and you should know that taking the Precepts formally is the meaning of lay ordination. This does not mean, however, that you never take the Precepts again. You can take them many times, every day as a matter of fact. It is customary for a trainee to put his kesa or token kesa on his head each morning and recite what is called the kesa verse:

> How great and wondrous are the clothes of
>     enlightenment,
> Formless yet embracing every treasure;
> I wish to unfold the Buddha's teaching
> That I may help all living things.[1]

The "clothes of enlightenment" are the Buddhist Precepts. They are the vehicle with which we penetrate the Truth and by which the Truth penetrates us. So after ordination, the first thing trainees do after their first meditation period of the day is to reaffirm their desire to keep the Precepts by reciting the kesa verse with the token kesa upon the head. And as I said in the beginning, the most important thing is to take the Precepts NOW—today—and worry about next week, next month, next year when it comes. The most important thing is to take them now because the only time you *can* keep the Precepts is right now. Therefore, to become a Buddhist is to receive the Precepts and then practice them. You will have to decide how deeply you are going to go, you will have to decide how far you are going to take them. The Buddhas only point the way; they cannot do your training for you. Only you can know when you have made a mistake, when you have broken the Precepts; and only you can decide that you are, nevertheless, going to continue to try to keep them. It is all up to you.

The next ceremony is called the Ceremony of Contrition and Conversion. It is the epitome of the idea of going into darkness and, from that darkness, into light. For those of you who have never done it before, I would like to explain a little bit about it. On the night of Contrition and Conversion, the ceremony begins with a period of meditation. When the gong is struck, the trainees line up and begin to process slowly along a very dimly lit path, chanting "Hail, Shakyamuni Buddha." We chant "Hail, Shakyamuni Buddha" because we are doing what He did. This, to me, is another great thing about Buddhism: it does not matter if you are a layman, it does not matter if you are a monk, it does not matter if you are a woman, it does not matter if you are a man. When you train you are doing exactly what the Buddha did, in exactly the same way.

In the first small shrine that you come to, there will be a priest who represents Avalokiteshwara, the Bodhisattva of Great Compassion. The priest will take a piece of paper, cense it and then hold it out to you. The paper is meant to symbolize all of one's karma. It is important to note that the priest will not give it to you; you have to decide to take it for yourself, just as when we meditate, our karma arises and it is up to us to decide whether or not we are going to do something about it. The priest will hold it out to you and if you wish to take it, please do so. You then bow and walk back out into the darkness. Further on, there is a second shrine in which another priest is sitting representing Samantabhadra, the Bodhisattva of Great Love, selfless love. Samantabhadra holds a bowl into which, if you wish, you put your piece of paper. Thus, you first recognize and accept your karma and then you give up all the ways in which you perpetuate it—you put your piece of paper into the bowl, bow and go out again into the darkness.

You continue on in the darkness, all the time chanting "Hail, Shakyamuni Buddha," until you come to a third priest who represents Shakyamuni Buddha. That priest will burn incense and make gasshō to each trainee who comes up, while in the background you hear the Contrition and Conversion verse.[2] Here it is shown that when you truly cleanse your karma you become a Buddha: this is the first sign of recognition, and the recognition is twofold. When a real act of contrition and conversion is done, *you* begin to get a sense of what a Buddha is. "Buddha recognizes Buddha and Buddha bows to Buddha."

The procession continues on in the darkness until it finishes in the ceremony hall. The three priests join everyone there, light each paper and burn them in a cauldron at the center of the hall. This fire expresses that time when the desire for training has become so strong, when the fire of our determination has become so strong, that the spirit of Immaculacy, of Buddha Nature, blazes up within us. The three priests of Avalokiteshwara, Samantabhadra and Shakyamuni Buddha again bow to all of you in recognition that this is what you truly wish to do, this is what you have done, and this is what you will do. The trainees return the bow, the ceremony is over and all return again to sit in meditation—you go back into darkness. The darkness is the darkness of facing oneself. Within that darkness, however, there are moments of certainty when one sees the Buddha and receives the teaching. These moments kindle one's faith; they give us the courage to go back into the darkness, and we eventually realize that the darkness is not really an obstacle. When there is darkness, there is darkness; and when there is light, there is light. You can learn from darkness just as well as from light. Remember, though, that it is a mistake to desire either the darkness or the light. *Desire* is the keynote here. Sometimes it is dark, sometimes it is light: both states are part of training and enlightenment.

The Japanese word *sange* has often been translated as "contrition." "Remorse" also touches it—remorse over the suffering that one has caused. Out of it, however, comes gratitude because when you meditate, you come to realize that there really is something wonderful within yourself and all around you, and that you don't have to hold on to this "stuff" any more. Many of us spend a lot of time holding on to the "devil" we know because we think it is a lot safer than the devil we don't know. In training, you have to step out into the unknown, you really have to take risks. Americans like to have everything laid out for them: "Yes, I have a contract to do this, I have my insurance policy, I'm all set to go, my life is secure." The weather this year has been a good teacher. Look at all the suffering and misery that it has created. It is another sign that all things are impermanent and no matter how perfect man becomes, suffering will exist. Therefore, it says in the *Rules for Meditation,* "Give up everything."

Many of you have probably thought, "Well, if I give up everything, does that mean I have to shave my head and become a monk?" The answer is that it may mean that—it meant that to me—but it does not *necessarily* mean that to you. We each find and express our training in different ways. Furthermore, to give up everything today will be different from giving up everything in five years, ten years, or twenty years because you continually go on in training; through the darkness of everyday life, you continually try to do something about yourself. When we realize that the only thing we truly possess is the certain knowledge of the Eternal, we understand Great Master Dōgen's words, "All I know for certain is that on my face there are two eyes and a nose." And if you ask me, "What have you learned in your twelve years in the monastery?", I would say that within everything there is an Unborn, Undying, Uncreated, Unformed, That which we call the Eternal. When we realize that we really do possess It, and when we have faith in It, when we live in It, we *can* give everything up gladly.

Giving everything up does not mean that when the child is crying we say, "Sorry, kid, I'm going to go off to meditate now!" That is not giving up everything! True meditation cannot be done for a selfish motive. Giving up everything means that we recognize that there is something greater than ourselves: we listen to It, heed It, live in It completely. It is not going to ask us to break the Precepts, It is not going to ask us to hurt another being; It will, however, ask us what we really want and it is important that we be ready with the answer. I know what my answer is, for me; each of you will have to find out what your answer is.

This brings us to the next ceremony, the Ceremony of Following Where the Precepts, as the Blood of the Buddhas, Leads. Only the day on which it takes place and not the time of the ceremony is announced. At some time on that day, the Master leaves her house very quietly and begins to walk towards the ceremony hall, softly chanting "Gyatei, gyatei, hara gyatei, hara sō gyatei, Bodhi, sowaka!" This is the last line of *The Scripture of Great Wisdom* meaning "Going, going,...always going on beyond, always BECOMING Buddha. Hail!"[3] You really have to be on your toes, and when you see the procession move, go to it, and join on the end. The procession winds and it twists and it turns and it doubles back on itself. The idea of following the old monk is the same as following one's heart, the Cosmic Buddha, following the Precepts through the twists and turns of everyday life. To do that, one has to listen very deeply to one's heart, listen for the call, heed it, say "Yes! I'm ready" and then follow it. All of us have our own karma to fulfill. Mine is to be a monk at the moment; yours, at the moment, is to be lay trainees, to take care of your families, to do your work, or whatever it may be. The Bloodline of the Buddhas is a representation of how to live in the world with all the difficulties, with a bright mind. Do not forget the "Hail!" at the end of the mantra! Training must become consistently bright. And that takes time, effort and experience for it can be hard to keep up that brightness—especially when it seems like the whole world around you is going crazy! But the Precepts and the Bloodline of the Buddhas show us how to live in the world.

*"Going on, going on, and always going on beyond, always* BECOMING *Buddha. Hail!"*

*Ketchimyaku,* itself, means "bloodline," the Bloodline of the Buddhas. The blood of the Buddhas is the Precepts: the Bloodline is their Transmission. In the ceremony hall during this ceremony, the master shows her Bloodline of the Buddhas silk that she received from her master and explains how the Precepts come from the Eternal, how they have gone through all the Buddhist Ancestors down to her at the present time, and now on to those of you who are taking the Precepts. Each person who takes the Precepts is added onto the Bloodline and is called a new ancestor, for simultaneous with the acceptance of the Precepts is their Transmission. The Precepts define the relationship between self and other such that when we keep the Precepts, we are already automatically giving them to others. We may not be conscious of it, but as one's training deepens, one comes to see that this is true.

On the last night of the Ten Precepts Meeting is the Ceremony of Recognition. At Recognition you are again sitting in darkness. In groups, the trainees are brought up onto the main altar from which they see, in the shrine of the Founders, the three Abbots, Avalokiteshwara, Samantabhadra and Shakyamuni Buddha. In Buddhist terminology, to climb Mt. Sumeru (which is represented by the altar) is to become Buddha. From the viewpoint of enlightenment, Buddha *does* recognize Buddha, and Buddha bows to all other Buddhas. Thus there are mutual recognition and gratitude. It is said that enlightenment is very much like a rope. When one strand does its job, it makes it possible for each of the other strands to do its job. The enlightenment of one person becomes the enlightenment of everyone. Shakyamuni sat beneath the Bodhi tree 2500 years ago and look at how His enlightenment has affected our present lives. *One* person trained Himself and became enlightened and think of what a great influence it has had and how it has been carried down through to today! It is truly amazing!

The Recognition ceremony recognizes the Buddha Nature, the Eternal, within each one of us. It is the jewel of faith. The interesting thing about faith is that it begins with doubt: we go along in life and all of a sudden, for whatever reason, we find that things don't seem to be right anymore. That doubt, that sense of incompleteness, makes us begin to look deeper into ourselves and what we do. That is what brings us to the monastery. As we work on doubt, it turns into belief because we find the Buddhist teaching and we begin to believe in it. It is not enough to believe in something, however, one has to have faith. Faith is taking belief a step further, for it is the intent and the practice of living to the *best* of one's ability. Belief is a passive thing; faith is much more active. It says in one of our offertories, "Wherever a True Heart exists," wherever there is a pure intention, there "the Dharma springs up also;...[4] It does not matter if the person is a fully enlightened Buddha or a street sweeper from Toledo, Ohio; where a pure heart exists, there is the Dharma. If we are really looking, we can see this Dharma being shown to us; and if we are really training, we can show it to others; we may not see it in ourselves but it will be there. Through faith, we eventually find that It is a reality: It becomes and is one's everyday experience. During the Recognition Ceremony, the entire universe, represented by the monks, celebrates in gratitude, for the Buddha has shown the Precepts to all living things and all living things have taken the Precepts and will take the Precepts, eternally.

* * *

*Notes.*

1. See Rev. Master P.T.N.H. Jiyu-Kennett, M.O.B.C., *The Liturgy of the Order of Buddhist Contemplatives for the Laity* (Mt. Shasta, California: Shasta Abbey Press, 1987), p. 58.
2. "All wrong actions, behaviour and karma, perpetrated by me from time immemorial, have been, and are, caused by greed, anger and delusion which have no beginning, born of my body, mouth and will; I now make full and open confession thereof." See ibid., p.26.
3. Ibid., p. 78.
4. Offertory for Founder's Day.

# *About Shasta Abbey.*

Shasta Abbey is a seminary and training monastery for the Buddhist priesthood under the spiritual direction of Rev. Master P.T.N.H. Jiyu-Kennett, Abbess. The Abbey provides religious training for both male and female members of the priesthood and a year-round program of religious retreats and services for lay trainees. For more information, please contact the Guestmaster at Shasta Abbey, P.O. Box 199, Mt. Shasta, California, 96067, telephone (916) 926-4208.